121 Ways Toward a More Effective Church Library

Arthur K. Saul

VICTOR BOOKS

a division of SP Publications, Inc.

WHEATON. ILLINOIS 60187

Offices also in Fullerton, California • Whitby, Ontario, Canada • Amersham-on-the-Hill, Bucks, England

Library of Congress Catalog Card Number: 79-92513
ISBN: 0-88207-171-8

VICTOR BOOKS
A division of SP Publications, Inc.
P.O. Box 1825 • Wheaton, Ill. 60187

To

My mother
who introduced me to life-changing guides
for my life:
the Saviour,
the Word of God,
and books.

Contents

Preface

Aim of This Book

This book will be dealing with methods for developing an effective library in your church. The book should be of service to three groups of people.

1. To help church members understand why their church needs a library.

Why is it that less than 50 percent of churches have a library? Why is it that 50 percent of churches that do have a library keep it virtually inactive? Many librarians have expressed the reason to me very simply, "No one in our church seems to realize the important role the library can have."

Since the beginning of church libraries, the majority of people in any given church has neither understood nor appreciated what the library is able to do for the overall ministry of their church. In many cases, library leadership that would help people grasp the importance of the library has been lacking.

As a result, indifference to the library ministry has been shown in several ways. The *space* usually given for library activities is insufficient. Often the library must share facilities with a class, use a room that is far removed from the line of traffic, or use one of the smallest rooms on the church property.

What a contrast to the space given to Sunday School rooms used only once a week, to youth activities serving only one segment of the church family, or to a well-equipped kitchen! Sufficient space for a library could result in a ministry that would instruct, edify spiritually and provide wholesome entertainment.

Indifference is also reflected in the amount of *finances* allotted. Many churches do not include the library ministry in their budget. If they do, the amount may be only enough to buy a couple of dozen books each year. Churches invest in hymnals to assist in worship; teacher and student manuals to assist in learning; and various kinds of equipment to assist in fellowship. Adequate finances would enable a library to purchase materials that could assist in every area of the church's ministry.

Little emphasis is placed on the importance of the library ministry in relationship to other church ministries. Ask a number of people in your church this question: "What do you consider the most important ministries of our church?" Most will reply, "The pastoral ministry, the teaching ministry or the music ministry." But few ever indicate the communicating ministry of the various media housed in the church library.

One more evidence that the library is not appreciated in the average church is that such a small percentage of people *use* the library. Your local Christian bookstore faces the same problem. Not more than 8 to 10 percent of the members of any given church visit a Christian bookstore. As a result, many people have no idea what God has provided for their spiritual development and use. They would be amazed to find out the great amount of materials available to them.

To develop and maintain an effective library requires a realization, not only by the library leadership but also by the majority of the people in the church, that a library can have a vital, spiritual ministry. You and I who have considered this ministry know it can contribute much to individuals for their Christian living and Christian service.

God often uses materials found in the library to serve His purposes. He has used books that contain:

Christian biographies to inspire teens to serve their Lord faithfully;

Doctrine to help students gain a better understanding of Bible truths;

Christian living concepts to challenge people to live a consistent Christian life;

Bible study to help God's people in their continued study of a book of the Bible; and

Fiction stories to show what God can do to meet the needs of everyday living.

Your church needs a library because it is a vital Christian ministry. It is a ministry made possible through:

Christian men and women to whom God has spoken and revealed a heart message; these messages being put on the pages of a book, the tape of a cassette, or an image on the screen; God's Spirit taking the message from the page, the tape or the screen and, through the eye or ear gate, applying it to the heart of the individual reading or watching; the dedication of library staff members who give person-to-person heart service to those who come into the library.

2. To help the church leadership lay foundations for a library that will have an effective ministry.

Too often someone gets the idea that his church needs a library, but because of lack of training or improper preparation, the library is never able to give the strong, spiritual service that it should.

This book was written to give guidelines for building a library that can minister to the entire church. Emphasis has been placed on the fact that the library ministry is great in scope, in service, and in responsibility. It takes dedicated, detailed work to make the library go. It will not be successful if operated by just anyone in any way.

3. To help church librarians develop their library so it will be better than it was and have a greater impact in the overall ministry of the church.

Ideas have been included that can be adapted to the particular needs of each library. As you read, remember much of the material is presented from an ideal library situation. This will give a high goal at which the librarian can aim.

The last 15 years have seen a constant increase in the number of libraries coming into existence. Seminars are usually well attended by people who are concerned about a library ministry for their church. But the need is not only for a growth in the number of churches developing libraries, but also for a growth in the quality of existing libraries.

A New Image for the Library

Until a few years ago, the words *small, limited,* and *uninteresting* described the average church library. Books comprised 99 percent of the materials that could be borrowed. Yesterday's church library had a very limited readership. Because of the lack of appeal to individuals and the inability to stir up interest, not too many came into the library. Yesterday's library was only a storehouse. The librarian chose the books, placed them on shelves, and waited for someone to come after them.

Today, more and more people are becoming aware that the library is a necessary adjunct to the educational program of the church. It is no longer the pet project of one person or one organization of the church, but rather is a progressive venture of the entire church. Today, a strong base is built and then the library reaches out to people where they are, seeking to minister to the entire membership.

A number of years ago, new descriptive names for public school libraries began to emerge. These names represented a concentrated effort to redefine the function of the library. Some of the names are given below to help us in our consideration of what a church library should be today.

Learning Center. This name says the library is a place to learn. The emphasis is on the use of materials in the library. Public libraries are learning centers in that they have materials that can not only be checked out for learning at home, but also can be used at study tables and listening centers along with the convenience of copy machines and a quiet atmosphere.

Today's church library should be able to make this learning opportunity available to the people of the church.

Resource Center. The library is a place to enrich learning. The emphasis is on the gathering of materials to give an in-depth understanding of biblical knowledge. An individual, therefore, can learn more about a certain subject through the use of printed and audiovisual materials that have been carefully selected.

Today's church librarians should be gathering materials to help people gain a better understanding of the truths of God's Word.

Instructional Materials Center. The library is a place to obtain materials to assist an individual in learning or teaching. The emphasis is on providing a central location for the best tools for communication (1) for different patrons, and (2) to be used at different times.

Today's church librarians should be concerned about helping people communicate God's message to others.

Enrichment Library. The library has materials that will enrich the lives of the users. The emphasis is on a deeper spiritual life and a fuller biblical knowledge. It has been said that a reading people is a growing people.

The church library should provide books and audiovisuals that will stretch and strengthen the soul.

Media Center. The library is a place where all types of media can be stored. The emphasis is on preparing and helping people use media for their own benefit as well as for others.

Today's church librarians should bring together as many media as possible and then motivate the people of the church to make use of the media.

Two terms used specifically about church libraries which help describe their functions are:

Christian Education Library. The library is an important factor in the teaching ministry of the church. The emphasis is on the library's vital role in the total Christian education program. The basic reason for its existence is to provide for both students and teachers instructional services and materials which will enrich the total effectiveness of the teaching ministry.

Church Resource Center. Analyzing this name, we can see three important factors:

First, the ideal library touches all areas of the *church: Sunday School*—books for students to read; books for teaching background; audiovisuals for communication; *Children's Church*—supplementary books; resource books; audiovisuals; *youth programs*—research materials; how-to books; *weekday clubs*—seed-thoughts for devotional talks; special lessons; *home*—materials for family worship; materials to meet the needs of the family members; *Vacation Bible School*—how-to books for new workers; enrichment and audiovisuals for teachers; *camp*—books for quiet time; how-to books for counselors; devotional and inspirational materials.

The ideal library provides a wealth of *resources* from which a patron can draw. God has provided innumerable materials for His people. Through the years, the librarian has selected certain materials especially to help meet the needs of the people of the church.

The ideal library is a *center*—available to all the people of the church, coming from all the organizations of the church, involving all the activities of the church. The library should be in a central location to effectively serve all.

11

Personal Observations

Men and women. It is my earnest prayer that God will burden more men to take part in the library ministry. Up to the present time, based on attendance at library seminars, 98 percent of all library workers are women. Thank God for all the dedicated women who have filled library positions. But men could add much to the furtherance of the ministry through their Christian influence. This book favors the feminine pronoun because of this majority in library workers.

On the use of this book. As you read the book, you may come to a subject and say, "I wish more had been said about it." True, no subject has been exhausted. Many of the chapters could be developed into separate books. However, if you refer to the index, you may find the subject treated elsewhere in the book. Major subjects have been treated in several chapters and from several angles. The bibliography also will help you find more information on certain subjects.

Other-than-book media. The average church library should have more than books media. The word "library" as used with public libraries is no longer synonymous only with books. In your public library, you will note other printed media such as the vertical file, magazines and newspapers. In addition, you will find audiovisuals in varying degrees. Church libraries today are interested in communicating spiritual truths through every medium available.

Differences in libraries. Libraries differ greatly in quality, quantity, personnel, space, finances and many other ways. Your needs will differ from someone else reading this book. You may have to adapt the materials presented and even grow into some of the various activities described.

Your suggestions. Through the years I have been helped many times by the ideas and suggestions of church librarians who are building effective libraries. Any suggestions that you have that would help improve the book and be of help to other librarians would be gratefully received. If we can be of assistance in answering any of your questions, please write. Address: Victor Books • P.O. Box 1825 • Wheaton, Illinois 60187.

Does your church have a library? If not, those who teach as well as those who learn in your Christian education program may be missing the benefit of valuable resources. Pray that God will guide the church leadership to the person or persons who can lay the foundation for an effective library.

If you have a library, may you read and be motivated to develop this important facility into its full potential.

1
A
Church Library's
Ministry

A church library is vital to the educational program of a church. Our goal here is to look more closely at the *ministry* of a church library.

Defining the Ministry

The church librarian's function is three-fold: (1) to prayerfully, carefully and systematically select materials to support the entire teaching ministry of the church and to serve the spiritual needs of individuals; (2) to classify, store and make available those materials (3) to motivate individuals of all ages to use the materials.

Key words of the definition are:

Function. This word implies action. *Webster's Dictionary* defines "function" as, "The natural, required, or expected activity of a person or thing." A room, a thousand books, hundreds of dollars worth of visual aids will do nothing for the church unless there is activity.

Circulation. This is a key word of the library. The library is not merely a showroom of materials; rather it is a study room. The books and audiovisuals are not merely a gallery for observation, but a depository of resources to be used in and out of the library for the spiritual benefit of people.

Church. The library should not be a function *of* some one organization or *for* one organization of the church. It is a function that should serve and be supported by all the organizations and activities of the church.

Responsibility. Those who operate a library have just as important positions as any Sunday School teacher. For the fulfillment of their responsibilities, library workers answer to the Lord as well as to the church.

Select. The amount of of materials God has provided for the ministry of the church is unbelievable. No church has enough money to buy all the materials available, or even all the materials wanted. As a result, selection becomes a very important factor in the building of a library.

Support and serve. The library does not exist for itself. It exists to support all the teaching ministries of the church—the Sunday School, the pulpit, the youth programs, Vacation Bible School, etc. They can all be helped through an effective library program. The library also exists to be of help in the spiritual birth and growth of individuals attending the church as well as those who live in the community.

Classify, store, make available. This part of the definition involves a lot of detailed work. To classify materials properly, the purpose of every item put into the library must be determined in relationship to the ministry of the church and the lives of the people.

Every item for circulation must have a "home" where it can be stored until it is requested. All the materials must be readily available to the people of the church. People must be able to find the library, get into the library, locate the materials they need, and then be assisted in checking them out.

Motivate. Library workers can do all of the preceding things and yet see little activity in the use of the materials. People have to be motivated, encouraged, and taught how to use the library. For this reason, promotion is vital to the continuing function of a church library.

Describing the Ministry

There are several ways to describe the ministry of the church library.

Practical ministry. The ministry of the church library might be compared to what secular libraries are doing. Three kinds of secular libraries may be considered:

The public library provides (1) free service, and (2) materials that are geared to the needs of the community. Since boyhood, I have made use of the public library. No one knows how many books I have borrowed through the years. Many were books I could not afford to buy—books that gave me insight into many subjects and entertained me. And it was all free!

The church library should provide the same two practical services. First, it should be free to all the people of the church to use. Second, it should provide materials that are geared to the needs of the people of the church.

The emphasis of the selection of materials for your library may be altogether different than that of another church library in the same town. The reason is that the needs of one congregation are different from those of another. That is why it is important for the librarian to know the people of the church, their spiritual needs, and what materials would be especially helpful for their spiritual development.

Another secular facility is the public school library. Two important factors in the operation of this type of library are (1) that it supports the curriculum being offered in the classroom, and (2) that it offers teachers another dimension in teaching. This kind of library makes valuable resources available to both teacher and students. Someone has said about a good school library that it is "a collection of many materials of learning—selected, organized, and administered for service to the students and faculty of the school."

Two more practical services can be offered by the church library. First, it should support the Christian education curriculums of its church. Churches have curriculums in Sunday School, Children's Church, and Vacation Bible School, to name a few. Second, a church library should be able to make resources available to teachers which will add to their effectiveness in teaching. Where else can the teachers go to get the needed resources without spending a lot of time and money? Library materials do an effective job of supplementing textbooks and courses of study.

Then there are special libraries like those developed for businesses to help employees from the top levels of management to the persons doing the seemingly most insignificant jobs. Materials are provided in such areas as personnel development, interpersonal relationships, and continuing education.

The church library can be of help to the workers of the church—board members, committee members, ushers, etc.—in their ministry. It can provide materials to help in the same areas as special libraries. To be a useful Christian leader, one must experience spiritual growth. The leader must know how to communicate with others. He must know how to improve his job performance. Proper training of personnel through the library ministry could prevent many problems.

Don't try to build your library just philosophically or numerically. Rather, build it with children, youth, and adults in mind. Build it with their spiritual needs in mind. Build it with the church leadership and ministry in mind.

Teaching ministry. Library workers must be teachers in three areas. Instruction needs to be given on:

How to use the library. Some of the subjects that can be covered in this area are: using the *tools* of a library such as the card catalog and reference books; understanding the *policies* of the library such as checking out procedures for borrowing materials, the length of a loan, and the responsibility of the borrower; recognizing the *value* of books and the care the library takes in preparation of the book as well as the care that must be taken by the user of the book; how to *use* the library with purpose, profit and satisfaction. The library workers must show the techniques of browsing and the selection of the right book for the need.

How to use books. Assist those at various age levels to develop their *ability* to read and comprehend Bible truths; develop reading as a leisure-time activity; find information for the readers' individual studies and spiritual needs; include reading in people's weekly and daily activities.

How to use audiovisuals. Help teachers communicate God's Word through teaching tools geared to their needs by: stressing the importance of audiovisuals; teaching teachers the use of audiovisuals; assisting teachers in the preparation of equipment when using audiovisuals.

Service ministry. Someone has said, "Service is the reason for the public library." The same thing may be said about the church library.

Unless the library performs service for the people of the church, it will cease to function.

Some of the services the library can perform are:

Availability: Selected materials are ordered, received, cataloged, processed for circulation, and made available for the people of the church; the library is manned by staff members who desire to respond to the needs of the people.

Guidance: Although the library is filled with all kinds of helpful materials, most people need someone to help them at the card catalog and guide them to the proper shelf. Many appreciate receiving suggestions about what would fit their needs the best.

Information. People want to know the current selections, what new books have come in and information about authors.

Motivation. When a staff member has motivated someone to use library materials, he has done a real service for that person. Without that motivation, a blessing may have been missed, a teacher may have lacked necessary help for preparation, or a student may have missed having a truth more clearly presented with an audiovisual. Loving motivation can pay for eternity.

Outreach. The staff reaches out—to people who are unable to come to the library; to people who know little or nothing about Christian truths; to people who are sick and shut in. The library must go out. It cannot sit still in a room. If people will not come to the library, the library must go to the people.

All-age ministry. Library services should be available to every age group:

Children. A special area can be provided in which children will feel comfortable to read and browse. To have a good children's section, books must be geared to the age-level of the children; a friendly and helpful staff must show special care for children; children must feel at home in the library. Giving special attention to children will build lasting relationships for the future.

Teens. Teens need access to the entire library. But books that provide answers to the needs of their lives; books that have stories with teen characters and familiar environmental settings; books that help with career guidance—can be grouped together in a special place.

Adults. Remember the men as well as the women readers. Keep in mind the differences in the needs of young adults, mature adults, and senior adults. (See chapter 12, Enlarging Your Ministry.)

Demanding ministry. Many demands are made on the library staff:

Detailed work. Working in the library demands a lot of detailed work. Most of it is behind-the-scenes work. Records must be completed, follow-up work done, due materials checked, books cataloged and promotion done, to name a few.

Knowledge of people. The library staff must know the people of the church. Knowing their needs, the staff can determine what materials will serve them best. The library of any given church should be built with materials that will meet the needs of the people of that church. This will be emphasized later in such areas as selection, cataloging, and promotion.

Faithfulness. Once a library is started, it must provide service consistently. No matter the kind of weather or the problems of staff members, the library must go on. The library needs workers who will be faithful to the ministry month after month, year after year.

Cheerfulness. Some library workers attract people to the library through their dispositions, while others hinder people from coming. A smile, and a word of encouragement, may mean more to a person than all the materials in the room.

Rewarding ministry. Using library materials can be a means of receiving blessings. Spiritual growth can be stimulated. Workers can be inspired. People of all ages can be helped to live the Christian life. Individuals can be motivated to make spiritual decisions.

(See in chapter 2, under Step 3, For the church, p.28.)

In speaking to His disciples, as recorded in Matthew 10:42, the Lord said they would be rewarded if they gave a cup of cold water in His name. Someone recognizing the need of a thirsty person, getting the water, giving the water, the person drinking and then going on his way, strengthened, is a picture of the library ministry.

The staff member sees the need of an individual. She finds the book to meet the need. She puts the book into his hand. The needy person drinks in the message and is helped spiritually. In that book is the water of refreshment or the milk of nourishment. This too will be rewarded by the Lord.

Another reward is to be able to share in the ministry of the pastor and other teachers through the materials in the library.

(See in chapter 2, under Step 3, For the library, p.29.)

When people of the church use the library, they can be better workers; they can be better Christians; they can be better equipped to receive the weekly teachings of the pastor and Sunday School teacher.

A third reward is that of saving money for the church. Teachers who are media-minded will do a better job in teaching if they have the tools. But media cost money. The pooling of audiovisuals as well as books will help individuals save money while providing those materials that will aid teachers in their ministry.

(See in chapter 2, under Step 3, For the church, p.28.)

2
Basic Steps
in Developing
a Library

Our primary purpose here is to help those who are interested in beginning a library ministry in their church. You will find the starting point and the steps that can lead to a solid foundation on which to effectively build a continuing library ministry.

This material also can be helpful for a library that has been in operation for some time, but is not going well. In this case, you would profit by reviewing each step. Should you find some of the steps have been omitted in the building of your library, try to incorporate the ideas into your future plans. If you are doing poorly in some of the areas described, work on improving those areas. Taking such action could make a big difference in the way your library progresses.

It is vitally important to lay a good foundation for your library ministry before you open it to the people of your church. To complete and have in operation all these steps before opening may delay the operation, but the extra effort will pay off in the long run.

Step 1. Discover a Key Person
The first step—the starting point, the place to launch your library—is with a key person, not with procedures or policies. Every successful

library requires a key person, who is the librarian. That key person must be discovered. God knows who it might be. Could it be you? Are you the one who has been called to be the key that will unlock the door to a library for your church? Whether you know it or not, if you *are* the librarian, you are the key person.

What are the characteristics of the librarian as the key person? She will be a person with:

A vision. In His own way, God leads an individual to see what a library can be. She catches a glimpse of what can be done through a church library. Her own reading has been a blessing to her and so she feels others could be blessed by the reading of books. Perhaps she has seen what other churches have been doing.

Whatever the source, she is aware of the blessings that can come through the library. Usually such a vision reveals only a small part of the scope of the library ministry and little realization of the vastness of the library's possibilities.

A call from God. God puts His finger on an individual and says, "That's what I want you to do. I've shown you what can be done; now I want you to be the one to do it." The key person has answered the call of God to fulfill His command.

A developing library is not built by a person thrown into library work by mere man, or by a person who reluctantly accepts the job. To be an effective librarian is as much an appointment from God as is a Sunday School teacher's call. God seeks those whom He knows can do the job. He has equipped them with the necessary gifts of the Spirit and with the talents needed to do the work.

A commitment. In response to God's call, one makes a commitment to Him to enter into this ministry. An individual might see that the library ministry is vital to the church; she could feel it ought to be done. But then she might say, "I'm too busy to do it myself, even though I see the need. We've got to get someone."

Until that person says, "I see what can be done; I'm convinced to the extent that I feel I should drop other things and commit myself wholly to this task," she does not become the key person.

A burden. One must have a burden to see that a library is started, to get people using the library for their own good. The key person knows the only way to handle the burden is to "cast it upon the Lord."

A sacrificial attitude. The librarian faces up to the fact that it requires sacrifice to do her job well. Her life will have to fit in with the library's needs. Time, money and effort must be willingly directed toward the library ministry. Other church jobs will have to be sacrificed, as much as she might like to do them. She must be willing to do anything she can to get the library ministry moving.

One word of warning: Be careful not to sacrifice time that belongs to fellowship with the Saviour, study of God's Word and care for our families. Letting up in any of these areas will result in an adverse effect on the librarian and the library.

Zeal. Because of her zeal for the ministry, the librarian will be able to inspire others with her enthusiasm. Her love for the library ministry will be communicated to others.

Training. A person may have all the characteristics mentioned, but without training much will be left undone. If the librarian must begin without training, she should give training priority in her plans for the future.

Practical training that can help a person be a good librarian includes the experiences of teaching a Sunday School class or working in an administrative area of church work; the patience of having done detailed work; and the enjoyment of reading.

Helpers. To be an effective key person, the librarian must have helpers. Even with a vision of what can be done, and the necessary training to do a better job, one can get so bogged down with the work load that the joy of the library ministry is lost. One's spiritual and physical condition can be affected.

(See in chapter 3, The Librarian, p.38.)

Step 2. Obtain Leadership Confirmation

If God has called you to be the librarian, the key person of the library, the church leadership must discover this also. An effective church library cannot be built without the backing and encouragement of the church leadership.

If the church board has discovered the library mininistry is important to the teaching ministry of the church, the board members must look for a key person. Being directed by the Holy Spirit in its selection, the board will officially appoint the librarian and work with her in the choosing and appointing of an initial library committee.

If the person whose heart is burdened for the ministry is the only one who recognizes the need for a library, she must approach the leadership of the church to present the value of the library ministry, her willingness to serve as librarian, her qualifications to serve as librarian, and the need for others to help on an initial library committee.

The initial library committee can consist of three to five members appointed for three to six months. Members can be chosen from the church board, the Christian Education Committee or a representative of a Christian education organization.

The librarian and the committee will then explore the possibilities of a library ministry in the church. The people of the congregation will be contacted. The leadership will be instructed about the library's possibilities.

Some church libraries in the area should be visited to see what other librarians are doing. People should be enlisted to help on a regular basis. A recommendation should be prepared for the leadership to examine and act on.

(See in chapter 2, Step 4, section about the church board, p.29.)

Step 3. Define Library Objectives

Once the church leadership has determined to have a library and has appointed the librarian and the permanent library committee, the librarian can take her place at the helm of the library and is ready for step three in the building process.

It is important that a set of objectives be formulated that will answer such questions as: Why do we need a library ministry in our church? What can be accomplished through this ministry? What are the priorities of the ministry? What are the specific results we want to see?

The objectives should be well thought out and then written out. They will act as a guide in the initial planning stage of the library. Later these objectives will provide information for the promotion of the library and help in the evaluation of the ministry. Objectives can be related in three ways:

1. For the individual people of the church. The librarian will want her library to be a person-oriented library seeking to reach everyone connected with the church.

The library should help people increase their knowledge of the Bible. Through library materials, people can become better acquainted with the Bible. They can take advantage of the teaching of outstanding Bible scholars, both contemporary and from the past (Prov. 13:20a).

The material can help provide answers to spiritual needs whatever they may be. It can also help the patron understand the facts, doctrines, geography of the Bible, and help him explain to others what he believes and why he believes.

Proper materials help stimulate spiritual growth among God's people. The library can provide materials that help in every phase of Christian living. Questions can be answered. Christians can be helped in making spiritual decisions about matters which challenge them.

Such tools assist people in Christian service. How-to books can be provided to help workers learn to do a certain job or do it better. Audiovisuals can help workers be more effective in their communications to others. These workers include: the pastoral staff, board members, committee members, leaders in Christian education, teachers, devotional leaders and ushers.

Too, these materials can bring the message of salvation to the unsaved. Christian fiction, books on salvation, and Christian biographies can lead people to think of what God has done for them in Christ. These books also can give direction on the current issues of the day. Many social issues—drugs, crime, abortion, astrology, etc.—challenge the believer for answers today.

Christian media can be made available to support the parental instructional program and provide uplifting entertainment for the home. So much that comes on television and radio is colored by the sins of society and is detrimental. Materials also can be provided to help in family worship.

Too, the library staff promotes the use of Christian literature. The library can introduce people to the wide realm of printed and audiovisual materials. It can help people to use books as companions in their study of the Word of God. It can help people to use books to provide wholesome and constructive entertainment.

The library can help people to use books as a substitute for the poor literature found all around them. The Christian goes into the average secular library and is presented with materials that have no connection with Christ or may even be antichristian. The church library offers materials on many of the same subjects found in the public library, but all from a Christian viewpoint.

Your aim would be to provide resource materials that will help supplement the Bible teaching people are now receiving, which will be adding to leaders':

Spiritual growth—effective service requires personal and rewarding spiritual growth.

Improved performance—how-to books can help workers learn to do a certain task or learn to do it better.

Communication with others—the other-than-book media have been used to help teachers better communicate God's message to both old and young.

2. For the church. The library does not exist for itself. It exists to support all the ministries of the church. The library should not be a function *of* some one organization or *for* one organization of the church. It is a function that is to serve and be supported by all the organizations and activities of the church.

It should support the curriculums of the church. The Sunday School, Children's Church and Vacation Bible School are the major users of structured curriculum. In addition many churches have teacher training classes, pastors' classes, an intern program, and an effective discipling ministry.

The materials in the library can supplement the materials being offered and thus enrich and improve each teaching program. Resources can be made available to teachers and students.

The library can provide a central storehouse for resources and supplies that can be used from year to year. These will be books that teach the philosophy of teaching; aids to help new workers; a church manual developed in a loose-leaf notebook that contains information for all aspects of all jobs in the church. When new people take over a job they can find help, direction and motivation to help them in their work.

Such material can keep leadership up-to-date with the changing world. The needs of individuals change. The patterns of church administration change. Educational methods, materials and philosophies change.

3. For the library. Goals can be set for circulation, number of books to be entered into the library, finances to be received to operate the library, and development of the staff.

Library skills instruction can be provided and presented throughout the church.

(See in chapter 1, Teaching ministry, p.18.)

Step 4. Enlist the Help of the Church Leadership

You are now at the point where God has called a key person to open the door of the library to the church. The board has appointed the librarian and permanent library committee. Together they have been working on a set of objectives to use as they approach the leadership of the church once more.

Begin by contacting the *pastor(s)*. Assure him that this ministry will support his ministry. Show him a copy of the objectives and ask him for any suggestions that he might have to improve them. When the pastor has been enlisted, he will be able to help in the presentation of the ministry to the church board and the congregation.

Next, the *church board* needs to be contacted. The written objectives and a list of potential services will reveal the value of the library to the church. They should be able to see that the library can benefit the total church ministry. If a library is to be started, the board must deal with several important matters.

The initial and operating costs must be considered. The church may not have $500 to $1,000 to give as the initial outlay for equipment, materials and supplies. A decision must be reached as to how this can be accomplished without hurting other financial commitments of the church.

In addition to an initial outlay, there is a need for monthly funding. The library should be on the church budget for a minumum of $25 per month. The librarian should promise a prepared library budget and regular financial reports. This might also be the time to get approval for people to designate gifts for the library in various ways. (See chapter 4, Finances.)

Housing for the library is important, too. The first choice for a room would include one that is easily accessible to the people of the church and would be used entirely for library purposes; also, one that people will see at least once on Sunday as they walk about the church property.

Less attractive choices would include sharing a room with some other organization or using a room in an out-of-the-way place.

(See chapter 5, Housing and Equipment, p.67.)

One other group of people you need to enlist might be called *library supporters*. The public libraries have a cooperating organization, "Friends of the Library." Local chapters help their library in many different ways.

For example, the general aim of the Fullerton, California Friends is to "promote an understanding of the library's resources and the library needs." The Tacoma, Washington Friends state as their aim, "A group of active and dedicated people who believe Tacoma should have the best in library services." Their common bond is the desire to support and promote a library system which provides cultural, intellectual and educational enrichment for the citizens of Tacoma.

A group of "friends" like this for your library could help other people of the church understand what resources are available in the library; they could help others to realize the financial needs of the library and urge them to help meet this need.

Because they are convinced the library ministry is important to the entire church program, they would work to make it the best possible library. They could sponsor a book fair, work on a special area such as the children's, build the reference section of the library, or buy some special equipment needed that is not in the budget.

Set a goal of 10 supporters to begin with. They can elect their chairman for the action committee. Keep them informed so they can work and pray with you.

Step 5. Recruit Personnel

Sufficient personnel is needed to make your library effective. If you, as the librarian, expect to do it all by yourself, you will soon become discouraged. The big job is to recruit people to fill the jobs. Therefore, it is important that you begin to look for people who can help you. How do you go about recruiting the necessary personnel?

Pray. Ask God to guide you to people to whom you can go. Enlist people to pray with you. Bring up your needs at prayer meeting as a prayer request.

Consult with leadership. Talk to the pastor, Sunday School superintendent, Sunday School teachers, youth leaders, and members of the board.

Personally interview people. When you approach a person, do not ask him for an immediate response. Leave a sheet with the job description as well as the benefits of the church library ministry. Ask him to read the material carefully and pray faithfully before giving an answer. If you are enthusiastic about the ministry, you will be more apt to get others enthused. Interviews may not always bear an immediate response, but God could begin to work in hearts.

Advertise the library through mimeographed or printed sheets to let people know about its ministry. If your church is in the habit of distributing a job questionnaire annually, be sure the library's needs are reflected in the survey. If the church does not do this, make your own questionnaire.

Make definite assignments when people respond. Take people for the times they can offer—every week; once a month; by the hour. Make a schedule and assign each worker the time and what you want her to do. Sit down with her and explain what needs to be done and how to do it.

Invite teens as well as adults to come in to be an assistant for a day. This will acquaint them with the library ministry. Train students young and soon they will appreciate the library ministry. Later they will want to work in it.

Recognize faithful workers publicly. Dedication of workers in an evening service is beneficial.

(See in chapter 3, People, p. 37.)

Step 6. Prepare the Assigned Room

Once you have space assigned to the library, it will need to be prepared to be used in the best way possible. A maximum amount of shelving on which to store and display books should be installed. Room will be needed for such basics as a service table or desk and a card catalog. Other things can be added as the library grows and more space becomes available.

Some suggestions for preparing the room: Study the room; measure the size; look for outlets; note any wall projections; note the condition of the walls; check the lighting. Draw a layout. Scale it 1/2" to one foot; show the basic equipment by means of cutouts. Place them in different ways on the layout to see how you can utilize the space to the best advantage. Make it inviting. Use bright colors, flowers, special decorations, and turn some of the books with colorful jackets face out.

(See chapter 5, Housing and Equipment, p. 67.)

Step 7. Purchase Basic Library Supplies

Many of the necessary supplies can be purchased from your local Christian bookstore. The balance can be purchased from one of the library supply houses listed in the back of the book, or your local stationery and business supplies store.

Supplies needed to catalog books: catalog cards 3" × 5"—white cards for books with no ruling; white cards with vertical rules and one horizontal rule; audiovisual cards with 3/16" color bands—red, green, blue, brown, black, orange.

Supplies needed to check out books: accession book and sheets; catalog guide cards—an average of 1 guide to every 100 cards; electric pencil—permanently heat seals marking into book spine, won't peel or rub off; plastic transfer paper, comes in white, black and gold; book labels—pressure sensitive labels can be used on spine under book jacket covers, available in four sizes; color bands for book cards—1/8" color bands to go across the top of the book card and identify special group classifications, available in blue, orange, green, red, black, yellow; book cards 5" × 3"; book pockets 3-1/2" × 4-1/4"; date due slips 3" × 5"; dater; ownership stamp—used to stamp library name in books.

White Catalog Card with No Ruling

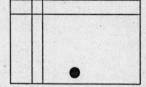

White Catalog Card with Vertical Rules
and One Horizontal Rule

DATE								
ACCESSION NUMBER	AUTHOR	TITLE	PUBLISHER	YR.	SOURCE	COST	REMARKS
01							
02							
03							
04							
05							
06							
07							
08							
09							
10							
11							
12							
13							
14							
15							
16							
17							
18							
19							
20							
21							
22							
23							
24							
25							

Accession Sheet

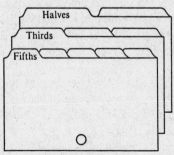

Halves

Thirds

Fifths

Catalog Guide Cards

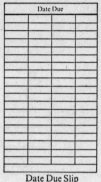

AUTHOR
TITLE

DATE DUE	BORROWER'S NAME

Book Card   Date Due Slip

Step 8. Begin a Selection of Materials

You are now ready to consider selecting media for the library. Someone has said, "A good library is made up of a selection of materials, not a collection." This is one of the most important functions of the library leadership—to get the proper materials for the people and the ministry of your church. The word "selection" as an acrostic gives us an insight into the subject:

S = *Specialized:* When you select materials for the library, you are specializing in materials that will fit in with the objectives of your library. There are many things that can be put in, but be choosy. You don't have the space, time or money to handle nonessentials.

E = *Educate:* It is necessary to educate the people of the church as to the way books are selected or accepted. Some people will want to give all of their old books and may not understand why they can't all be put into the library. Some may want to go out and buy books they like, presuming everyone will like them. Developing a selection policy will help prevent such problems.

L = *Library Committee:* The consensus of three or more people in the purchase of books can improve selection. Acceptance or rejection of materials offered by the people of the church will be much easier with a library committee than if done by one person. It is much easier to blame an individual than a committee because a book has been rejected.

(See in chapter 3, The Library Committee, p. 46.)

E = *Economy:* Make sure there is careful management of money. Select the best dollar profitability. First, consideration should be given to materials with wide usage. Ask yourself how much potential there is for the use of the book or audiovisual.

Watch for sales in your Christian bookstore.

Collect materials that are free: pictures, photographs, slides, tracts, clippings for the vertical file.

Keep track of your materials and avoid the needless expense of replacing lost items.

C = *Consultation:* Keep in touch with the church leadership for suggestions for the selection of books. They can give you ideas about materials that will be needed as well as help you understand the needs of people they have contacted.

T = *Test:* This refers to a standard or criterion by which the quality of a thing is tried. There should be a standard for the purchase of materials. All materials should be studied and selected according to these various standards.

(See in chapter 7, Prepare a Book Selection Policy, p. 103.)

I = *Inform:* Let people know what you have selected. People are always interested in anything new.

O = *Observe:* Spend time in your Christian bookstore browsing; ask for book catalogs and brochures; watch ads in Christian magazines. Observing books and information on books will help in the selection of materials.

N = *Needs:* Find out what the needs of the people of your church are. Buy on the basis of those needs.

Step 9. Classify and Catalog Materials

To classify means "to arrange or group in classes according to some system or principle." The question arises, what group classification should be used for books? Church librarians have chosen to classify books anywhere from a homemade system to a highly sophisticated system. In chapter 8, we will discuss the favored Dewey Decimal System. Then in chapter 11 a symbol/number system for audiovisuals will be introduced.

Step 10. Set Up Library Policies

Answer such questions as:

Who can use the library? Can members of the church; anyone who attends Sunday School; anyone who attends any function of the church; friends in the surrounding community?

When can the library be used? What hours do you plan to have the library open—before Sunday School, between Sunday School and church, after the morning service, before the evening service, during the week?

What may be taken out of the library? Can anything be taken out or are there some things on a reserve basis and qualified loan basis?

How long can books be retained? Can they be renewed? Will a fine be charged for past due books?

(See in chapter 3, Operating Policies, p. 48.)

Step 11. Promote the Library

Promotion is a continuous thing. From the time the library opens on its dedication day, people must be informed about the library. Promotion and the circulation of materials have a direct bearing on one another.

(See chapter 10, Promotion, p. 135.)

3
Administration

As you look at the administration of the library, you should take into consideration three areas:

1. *People*. It is people who make a library possible, practical, and valuable.

2. *Policies*. These are statements of operation which must be understood by both library workers and users if the library is to work most effectively and efficiently.

3. *Planning*. Unless you know where you are going and make plans to get there, you have no hope of ever arriving.

People

Libraries need more than one person to become successful just as any other ministry of the church does. No one expects the pastor to do everything that needs to be done in order to have a successful church. He must have the help of many people. When members leave their responsibilities at the door of the pastor, the church loses ground.

No one expects the Sunday School superintendent to do everything that needs to be done in order to have a growing Sunday School. He must have the help of many people. When people do not perform their assigned tasks or do them poorly, the Sunday School does not grow.

Similarly, church libraries must have the help of many people if the library is to develop into a function of the church that can be of service to every person and organization. One librarian cannot do it all. Without dedicated assistants, there will be a very limited development.

The ministry of the library cannot be computerized so that just a mechanical service is offered. The library is a service organization assisting people. All library workers must be concerned with serving and satisfying people. Service is a key word of the library ministry and only people can provide it.

Following, you find at least nine different positions listed that can be filled in a developing library to one extent or another. Many will look at the list and say, "That's wishful thinking. I'm here by myself. If something needs to be done, I'm the one who has to do it." As is the case when there is so much to do and so few to do it, many librarians in the same situation get frustrated, discouraged, and are unable to do the job they want and need to do.

If you are the librarian, the only library worker, you have a lot of things to do. You should go down the list and determine the things you feel are the most important. The rest will have to be let go. However, the more that is let go, the slower will be the total development of the library and this possibly could lead to a virtual standstill.

If there is no library committee, every effort should be made to form such a committee. With a minimum of three people taking an active interest in the library, most of the jobs can be done.

Study the following for the positions to be filled in a growing library.

The Librarian
The librarian is the executive head of the library. Her responsibilities include:

Supervising all library activities. She is in charge of the entire library operation to see that it is run properly.

Representing the library's activities. The activities of the library should be kept before the Christian Education Committee and/or the church board. They should know what is being done, what services are being performed and how God is using this ministry. They should be kept informed as to what is planned for the next quarter or month. Also, whenever any organization of the church needs the help of the library, there must be one person with authority to whom they can always go.

Training. If the librarian has had either formal or experiential training, she should share her knowledge with the staff. Time is wasted and development does not take place as it should when workers do not know what to do or how to do the job assigned.

Conducting staff meetings. Part of the training can be done in staff meetings. In addition to training, other worthy goals for staff meetings can be planning, evaluation and encouragement. If you have two or more people working with you, consider meeting with them monthly. Plan each meeting well even if it is for only a few people. Time is valuable to anyone who will be helpful to the library ministry.

Coordinating the selection of materials. As suggestions are received and research is done in preparation for the selection of books, the librarian will guide in the final selections. Selection is a difficult and somewhat technical task and must be directed by someone who has a knowledge of people, materials, and the church.

The librarian needs training in four areas:

1. Church practice and doctrine. It is important for the librarian to be able to build a selection of books that will support the church ministry rather than cause problems.

2. General Bible truths. It will help greatly if the librarian has a good understanding of the Bible as a whole, Bible history, Bible geography, basic doctrine, etc.

3. The characteristics of people. This will help her understand the needs of people at various age levels and she will be able to make the proper recommendations regarding materials that will be valuable for those who come into the library.

4. Library principles and practices. Through reading books, audiovisuals, and attending library seminars, the librarian can learn more about every phase of the library.

(See in chapter 2, Step 1, Discover a Key Person, p. 23.)

The Assistant Librarian

Every librarian, if working alone, should be praying for and looking for an assistant librarian. This person would be more than a helper. She would actually be preparing to take over if the librarian felt it necessary to give up her work for one reason or another.

Some of the saddest situations with regard to church libraries arise when there has been no assistant. A dedicated librarian finds she is unable to continue the ministry. A month passes, sometimes a year or even several years. During this time, the library sits useless, wasting God's money and depriving people of the blessings that could be received. But there is no one to head it up, no one who knows how to do the job. No one has caught the vision or is willing to help.

Responsibilities of an assistant librarian include:

Supervising the library in the absence of the librarian. The librarian should train her assistant in the various areas of the library. Then when vacation, sickness or other absence comes, the assistant can take over. The activities of the library can be kept in motion. Details will not pile up. Through this training and experience, the assistant can be prepared to take over the leadership of the library—if necessary—with confidence.

Keeping informed. The assistant librarian should keep abreast of new materials and offer suggestions as to what should be considered for selection. Her eyes should be trained to look at magazines, catalogs and brochures to see what materials are available. Her ears should be trained to listen to what is being said on Christian radio and television about books. She should listen to what the people of the church say they need.

One job could be to alternate with the librarian in visiting the local Christian bookstore about once a month to become acquainted with new as well as older materials. Suggestions should be compiled and brought to the library committee meetings for a careful review and consideration when selections are being made.

Representing the library to the church and its organizations. As much help as possible is needed to keep church leaders aware of the library ministry—its possibilities, its usefulness, how the church leaders can use it, what they can do for its ministry.

Inventorying supplies and media. This includes the supervision of two inventories:

Library supplies need to be inventoried on a regular basis. Running out of supplies for cataloging books or preparing promotion can slow down the work.

The media itself should be inventoried annually. The inventory will reveal what materials are in the library. The book cards will reveal what books are out on loan. These records should be checked against the total media record to provide: a list of any missing books to be traced for recovery; a verification of the value of the library at the point of the inventory; vital information to be included in reports to the church as to the value of library materials.

The total media inventory record can be kept in two ways. It can be kept entirely in an accession book. Or it can be kept on shelf cards. These records should be kept in the library room only if they can be protected from damage.

(See in chapter 6, Purchase the Book Selected, p. 89.)

Clerical Workers

Although clerical workers are not involved directly in administration as are the librarian and her assistant, they can make the load lighter in handling much of the detailed work. People are needed to:

Type. Catalog cards, book cards, overdue reminders, notices, stencils, monthly lists, reports, etc., need good typists. People are needed to type promotional copy for the printed media and to be responsible to prepare the necessary layout and have it ready to be mimeographed or printed. Look for high schoolers as well as adults who can type. (See in chapter 9, Typing the Cards, p. 129.)

Keep financial records. An accurate record should be kept of all receipts and disbursements. All financial transactions should be recorded. Regular financial statements, no matter how small the money involved, should be submitted to the church. This shows fiscal responsibility and encourages the church to entrust the library ministry with more money. (See chapter 4, Finances, p. 57.)

Keep vital statistics. A compilation should be made of materials checked out, materials purchased, the number of people coming into the library, and those who have been helped. A creative administrator should not be burdened with this detailed work.

Work at the service desk. In the church library, the service desk usually combines the work of several of the "desks" of the large public libraries such as the check-out desk, registration desk, return materials desk, information desk, and reserve desk.

When on duty, the staff member should try to ascertain the tastes and interests of those coming in. She should also make sure that all materials are checked out properly. If preschool children want to check out books, an adult should be involved.

Those who come into direct contact with patrons need to develop these characteristics: *smartness*—being able to answer questions and find out things for people; *smiles*—how important for library personnel to be cheerful.

Process materials. This includes putting book pockets, book cards, date due slips and, if necessary, bookplates in each book. Accession numbers, if used, and classification numbers need to be put in the book also. The library's name should be stamped in each book. (See in chapter 6, Process the Book, p. 95.)

Repair books. Pages that are torn and covers that are damaged need to be repaired. Books should be kept as clean as possible.

Follow up. Booking cards need to be checked for overdue materials and overdue cards sent. It may also be necessary to phone people regarding the materials they have borrowed. (See in chapter 3, Operating Policies, p. 48.)

Housekeeping. Church libraries should be kept neat and clean. Dirt should not be allowed to accumulate. Books should be placed neatly on the shelves, some with the face out. Floors should be kept clean. Light fixtures should be clean and in working order.

Evaluators

These are days when covers of books are made extremely attractive in order to motivate people to buy. Sometimes jackets and covers tell very little about the contents of the book. Doctrine and Christian ethics are very important when considering the library in its role of supporting the teaching ministry of the church. Evaluators can be very helpful in:

Evaluating each book in the light of the church's doctrine and its stand on Christian ethics. Such an evaluation would help the library committee to determine the type of endorsement that should appear in the book. (See section on The Library Committee, p. 46.)

Summarizing the book. This information would help the promotional chairman in the preparation of copy for printed and display material. It could also be of help to the cataloger in her gathering of information to put on the cards of the catalog. (See chapter 9, Information for the Catalog Cards.)

Cataloger
Here is a job that needs to be done by a person who is willing to specialize in this one task. She should have good judgment, church background and some Bible training. She is responsible to determine the correct classification number; prepare the main entry card for the typists; keep the catalog up to date.

The more a cataloger can characterize the materials in a book, the more valuable the contents will be to more people. (See in chapter 9, Tools for Cataloging, p. 123.)

Promotional Chairman
Because of the important part promotion plays in the development of the library, a promotional chairman should be obtained as soon as possible. The people of the church need to know what the library has, how it can help them and the services it provides. The library must be kept before the people so it becomes a part of their thinking when they consider the ministry of the church and their own lives.

Some responsibilities involved in this position are to:

Develop good public relations. This is saying to people, "We need you; you need us; we can help you; you can help us."

Provide displays and posters. Related books should be taken from the storage shelves and displayed. This sharpens the focus of people and helps them see valuable materials on an array of subjects for their use.

Posters are needed to support displays, give general library information and challenge people to use the materials. Young people and adults with artistic ability can build displays or make posters to place around the church property.

Prepare copy for printed materials. Many types of promotion can be done through the printed page. It takes someone to devote time to prepare copy that will be well written and placed in the hands of the proper people for printing.

Make presentations. The promotional chairman should see that visits are made to the Sunday School departments, the midweek service, the men and women's fellowship meetings, etc., to keep them informed about the library in a more specific way.

(See chapter 10, Promotion, p. 135.)

Audiovisual Librarian

As the library grows, both the printed media ministry and the audiovisual media ministry would be helped through the appointment of someone to give special attention to audiovisuals. These are expanding media with exciting possibilities, and time and effort should be given to them. Responsibilities of the audiovisual librarian include:

Making recommendations. As the scope of materials to be selected for the library grows, it becomes even more important to have someone who can spend time noticing and inspecting audiovisuals with the Christian education program in mind. He should be someone who spends time in learning the values, the use and the upkeep of audiovisuals. Careful consideration must be given as to what is best to help the workers of his church. After his evaluation, recommendations can be made to the library committee.

Training teachers. Teachers must be trained in the use of audiovisual equipment and materials, technically called hardware and software. Some teachers do not know how to use audiovisuals and therefore they make no effort to use them in their teaching. Some do not know how to use them, and yet use them without making the best possible use of the media. Then others have damaged equipment and materials by not using them properly.

A need exists for a trained person to take time to help all of the above. Training should be: (1) for motivation to use; (2) demonstrating how to use; and (3) developing an appreciation for equipment and materials.

Preparing and operating equipment. The pastor, a teacher, a departmental superintendent, or some other leader may need the assistance of a library worker to help them with their audiovisual presentation by operating the equipment. Equipment not properly operated can hinder or even nullify the lesson. The audiovisual librarian should work to be an expert in the knowledge and use of equipment.

(See chapter 11, Non-book Materials, p. 155.)

Assistant Audiovisual Librarian

As the use of audiovisuals grows and more people recognize the importance of using these media, the audiovisual librarian will need help. Just as an assistant is essential for the librarian who can take over when the need arises, so there is a similar need for an assistant audiovisual librarian. The responsibility of the assistant includes:

Maintenance of equipment. If audiovisuals are to be used efficiently and effectively in Christian education, they must be maintained properly. Filmstrip, slide, movie and overhead projectors must be checked regularly to see if they are operating properly. Such chores as checking lamps, cleaning lenses and cases, checking for broken cords and cleaning recorder heads need to be done on a regular basis.

Providing audiovisual information. It is easy for one person to get into a rut, or be limited in the time needed to improve his knowledge of a subject. The assistant can specialize in watching the development of audiovisuals especially by suppliers involved in Christian education. In this way, he can strengthen the ministry of both the audiovisual librarian and himself by sharing information.

Assisting in the operation of equipment. He would fulfill any requests assigned to him by the audiovisual librarian.

Library Representatives

These members of the staff are enthusiastic people scattered throughout the various departments of the Sunday School and other organizations of the church. They can be very useful in helping people make full use of library materials especially geared for the needs of the members. Because they are in direct touch with members of their groups and can get a feel for their needs, they can make suggestions to the library committee that will help in a better selection of materials. Duties of representatives include:

Inspiration. Each representative would bring to the attention of his departmental superintendent or organization leader what the library has to offer in study resources, how-to instruction and personal enrichment materials. He would encourage the leadership to motivate his workers to use the materials and thus make that department more effective.

The representative would also bring to the attention of the members the blessings and pleasure the materials in the library can be to them and their families. Through such information and inspiration, the representative could have a tremendous ministry that would supplement the structured teaching of the group.

Age-group specialization. The representative would be alert to materials available for the age group. He would be aware of materials wanted and needed by the people. He could be helpful in seeking to meet his organization's needs. He should be willing to cooperate with any special events sponsored by the group.

Satellite supervision. If a satellite library is put in the department or organizational room, someone must be responsible to see that the materials are checked out properly and returned on time. The representative will also be responsible for the transfer of books from the main library. He can work with the promotional chairman on effective ways to promote the materials selected for the satellite. He can also work with the audiovisual librarian to encourage the use of audiovisuals by teachers.

The Library Committee

The library committee is the governing body of the library. Its responsibilities include:

Preparation of all library policies. The committee should consider what policies are needed and then formulate them. Yearly the policies should be reviewed to see whether they are being of help to the library ministry and whether they can be improved.

A library manual should be developed by the committee. The manual will reflect the policies and procedures that will be peculiar to their library. The manual should include such things as:

A statement of the purpose of the library; organization and structure of the library; media to be included; services to be provided; library rules; instructional information for new workers; staff responsibility; a guide for classifying and cataloging books, and typing cards for the card catalog; a list of records to be kept; a selection policy.

Personnel responsibility. The committee should consider the needs for people to staff the library. It should determine the responsibility for each position. It should consider potential workers.

Planning all activities. It is one thing for the librarian to have a vision of what can be done through the library ministry. It is another thing for all the members of the committee to have the same vision. Without planning for the future, the library ministry will grow stagnant or may even cease.

Control the finances. For each fiscal year, a budget must be prepared. The committee should estimate the possible income for the year. Then priorities should be determined as to what should be purchased with the income. The money must be divided for books, audiovisuals, equipment and supplies. Such planning can prevent overbuying, show fiscal responsibility and help keep a proper ratio of spending in the various categories of materials.

Endorsement of books. After books have been evaluated, the recommendations should be considered by the committee in order that an endorsement code can be put on the booking pocket. Such a code could use the following designations:

A—Full endorsement of the book, the contents of which are compatible with the doctrine and Christian ethics taught by the church.

B—Partial endorsement—certain marked areas cannot be endorsed.

C—Non-endorsement—on the grounds that the contents are contrary to what the church teaches. The book is made part of the collection only for its comparative purposes.

Conduct a regular evaluation. The committee's evaluation will enable them to review not only what is happening, but also how it is happening. Committee members should look at the library as the people of the church look at it. They should try to determine how the library is or is not affecting the life of the church. After each evaluation, a plan of action should be formulated that will help improve the library. (See in chapter 13, Time to Evaluate, p. 183.)

Because of the importance of the library to the entire church program, it would be good for the church board to appoint the library committee. If the library is in its beginning stage, two church members could be appointed temporarily in addition to the librarian. The appointments could be made in various ways:

The board could make the actual appointment of the librarian and the committee; the board could ask the Christian Education Committee to make the appointments; the board could ask the congregation to vote on the librarian who in turn would appoint the other two members of the committee. (See in chapter 2, Step 2. Obtain Leadership Confirmation, p. 25.)

In the light of the need for so many workers in the library, where do you find people to do the work?

From the ranks of those who responded to motivation. You have challenged people with the importance of the library ministry and how they can help. You have repeated your challenges throughout the year through your promotion. Above all, you have prayed for God to touch the hearts of people.

From a list of possible workers which you have pursued. You asked for suggestions from the pastor and Sunday School teachers in addition to developing your own contacts.

You have contacted teenagers, individuals in adult organizations, shut-ins.

Operating Policies

Operating policies are rules to keep library services efficient. Without them the staff would not be able to do their best.

Included in the policy should be statements regarding:
Library users. Who will have the privilege of using the library?

Most churches invite those who are members of the church as well as members of the Sunday School to use the library. Others have opened the use of the library to any person attending one or more functions of the church. Some have even extended the privilege beyond the church to friends and neighbors in the community.

Church libraries should consider using library cards. Such cards are:
Reminders of responsibility. When a family registration form, along with the librarian's letter, is presented to parents, it will remind them of the privilege their family has in using the library and their responsibility

Suggestions for a Library Policy Sheet

1. *All members and friends* of the church are invited to use the library. A registration form is available from any member of the library staff.
2. *All books* with the exception of those in the reserve section may be borrowed. No more than two circulating books may be checked out at one time. Reserved books may be used in the library.
3. *Circulating books* may be borrowed for a period of two weeks. Books are to be returned or renewed at this time.
4. *Projected visual aids* may be borrowed only by those who have received training in the use of the equipment. Library personnel are available to instruct those who are interested.
5. *Audiovisuals* may be taken out one week ahead of their use and then are to be returned as soon as possible after their use.
6. Materials may be *checked out* whenever a member of the library staff is on duty. Our staff is on duty at the following times:
7. To promote *good stewardship,* those who do not return or renew books after two weeks will be asked to donate 25¢ per week to the library to help with the purchase of new materials.
8. Those who *lose or damage* materials beyond repair will be asked to donate the cost of the item to the library.

for return of the materials they borrow. The same form can be used for singles in the church with a different letter that will fit the situation.

A promotion of library services. After the form is returned to the library, the library cards for each member of the family can be prepared and distributed in the proper departments of the Sunday School. Depending on the expiration date (one or two years), the library would be promoted on a regular basis.

A tool for personal introductions. When cards are used, they help the library staff to refer to individuals by name. This can make a great impression on those who come into the library.

A help to insure correct records. The family registration form will show the correct names of all the members of the family. The family address will be helpful if promotional mailings are sent. The age bracket

FAMILY LIBRARY REGISTRATION CARD

Family name			
		S.S. Dep't.	Kind of books preferred
Father's name			
Mother's name			
Childrens' names			
Family address			

Family
card no.＿＿＿＿＿ Expiration date＿＿＿＿＿

Church Library Card
for

＿＿＿＿＿＿＿＿＿＿＿＿＿＿＿

Present this card each time you borrow a book.
You are responsible for all materials borrowed on this card.

Operator of visual aid equipment

＿＿ Cassette recorder   ＿＿ Overhead Projector
＿＿ F.S. Projector   ＿＿ Other

No. ＿＿＿＿＿＿＿   Card expires ＿＿＿＿＿

and kind of materials in which each person is interested will be helpful to those who are responsible for the selection of materials.

A means of making inter-library cooperation possible. Should several church libraries work together to make their materials available to the people of all the cooperating churches, a card would be needed so that those unfamiliar with an individual from another church would have the correct name, the name of the church and the card number of the individual. (See in chapter 5, Cooperative Church Libraries, p. 80.)

Library Hours
The following hours are typical of those observed by church libraries and are listed according to their priority:

Sundays—before Sunday School, after Sunday School, after the morning service, before the evening service, during the Sunday School hour; midweek—before and after the midweek service; special nights—30 minutes before and after special meetings such as missionary conference, evangelistic campaign, etc.; 15 minutes before and after club meetings, women's meetings, church socials; Saturdays—morning hours for children and others who might want to use the library; daily—especially if a Christian day school is involved.

In general, the library can best serve by being open 15 to 30 minutes before and after all services. However, each library must determine what works best for them. A limited staff should not be overloaded. Only hours should be kept that the staff is able to maintain.

When service is not offered, the library should be closed and locked. Materials should be taken from the library only under supervision to insure proper circulation. Of course materials can be returned at any time if a special receptacle is provided such as a slot through the door or a box outside the library room.

Library Loans
Materials to be loaned include books and audiovisuals. The two main categories of books are reference books which generally do not leave the library, such as atlases, commentary sets, concordances, dictionaries and Bible translations; and circulating books—those which may be checked out according to established policies.

Some libraries allow all audiovisuals to be borrowed by any library user. Others have user limitations such as allowing only teachers who have gone through an orientation to learn how to use delicate equipment.

Quantities to be loaned may differ from one library to another. Occasionally reference books are checked out by prior permission from the librarian because of unusual circumstances. Circulating books are loaned in quantities from 2 to 6. Limitations as to the number are made if the total number of books in the library is small or if there is a great demand for books on a certain subject. Audiovisuals should be taken out one at a time. The cost of materials and equipment, the limited supply and the value of materials make this necessary.

Procedures in loaning. How are books to be checked out? A number of libraries use the self-service system to one extent or another. There are two drawbacks to this procedure. One is the danger of patrons not making the proper records when taking out materials. The other is that Loving Library Service (LLS) is not provided. LLS is an important ingredient in the developing of a library ministry.

Procedure for self-service. Simple; definite instructions must be provided for patrons to follow. They can be put on a sign or poster where they will not be missed. Supplies for checking out books must be provided—a pen for writing the name on the book card and the date on the date due slip; a box to receive the signed cards. It would be well to set limitations as to who can borrow books on a self-service system. Audiovisuals should be taken out only through full service.

Procedure for full service. The personal touch includes helping the patron to check out the book. It would be well for the staff member to inquire as to what kind of books the reader likes, the books in which he has been disappointed or blessed. It would also include giving a word of promotion concerning a new book or books that have recently been received.

Combination of services. Loving Library Service can be provided for peak periods and self-service for other times.

Length of Loan. How long can materials be kept? Generally speaking, libraries loan books for a period of from one to four weeks depending on the number of books on hand and the circulation demand:

Books for pleasure reading—2 to 3 weeks with renewal privileges;

books for extended study and training—as long as needed; new books with a heavy demand—one week, no renewal; books for vacation—for the duration of the vacation; grace period—an extra week or 10 days beyond the date marked on the date due slip before the overdue time starts.

Overdue Materials

The date stamped on the date due slip is a commitment date. Patrons who keep materials beyond that date without contacting the library have overdue books. All overdue materials should be traced within three days and the borrower reminded of his responsibility to return or renew the materials.

If you do not show this concern for your materials, you give the impression that you don't care what happens to them. It does not reflect an obedience to the admonition to "do all things decently and in order" (1 Corinthians 14:40). Encouraging people to discipline themselves in returning books on time is a practical exercise in good stewardship of God's materials. When books are not returned on time, someone may be deprived of using them. The longer a book is overdue, the easier it is for the book to get lost.

A positive approach to overdue materials could be stated this way, "The first two weeks are free. After that, without renewal, the cost for using the book will be 10¢ per week (or whatever amount you set)."

Here are suggestions for the follow-up of overdue materials:

If it is known that the borrower has faced some extenuating circumstance, extend the due-date by renewing the book and notifying him. Also a valuable service could be offered if another book could be taken to the individual and the overdue book picked up.

If the circumstances are unknown, send a reminder card within three days.

If no reply is received in seven days, telephone the borrower to make sure he has the book. Sometimes the book may have been loaned to someone else.

If the book continues to be overdue for a month, arrange to have it picked up if possible.

Extreme action would include sending a bill for the overdue amount for the month; listing overdue books with the replacement cost of each in the church bulletin. Consult with the pastor as to the next course of action.

It is important that tact be exercised when contacting people regarding overdue materials. Do not try to force a borrower to return a book or pay a fine. Hard feelings could develop and perhaps the person might be lost to the Sunday School or church. It is better to lose a book than a person. Children can be helped in the lesson of stewardship by paying overdue fines through work in the library if they are unable to pay with cash.

It is good to determine as part of your policy the use to be made of monies received from overdue books. Libraries purchase new materials, replace materials, buy supplies or use the money for general operating expenses. Many borrowers feel that fines are an opportunity for them to contribute to the library and will give more than required.

Lost or Damaged Materials
Some libraries make no claim for lost or damaged materials in addition to not setting a fine for overdue books. However, the same reason made for requesting a fine for overdue materials would apply to those materials lost or damaged. Exercise the same tact.

Library Gifts
Part of the operating policy should include a statement regarding the receiving of materials from individuals. All items offered to the library should be reviewed by the library committee or those appointed to do reviewing. No library committee should be expected to accept and put into the collection automatically anything that is offered.

A number of reasons for this can be cited. The item may be in the library already and more of the same is not needed. The contents may not be acceptable for your church's use. The condition of the item may be too poor to use. It may be damaged beyond repair. It may not be an item needed for a church library. It may be out of date.

Every donated item should be carefully evaluated in the light of the library ministry. Books and audiovisuals should be screened according to the selection criteria. Just as with new books, meaningful selections should be made.

Have an understanding with the giver that one or all of the items may be rejected if the library committee comes to that conclusion after inspection. Also determine what disposition should be made of the items that are rejected.

It is best not to encourage the giving of any books to the library where the giver becomes the selector of the book. Help people to understand that the choice of books is the responsibility of a trained selector and her associates. A person who desires to purchase a book for the library should do so only with the help of the selector.

When operating policies have been formulated, publish them in a concise form for general distribution. A bookmark, dodger or manual can be printed for this purpose.

Planning for the Future

Although often omitted from library practice, planning is a very important part of library administration. Consistent planning is time well spent. If a library is to develop as it should, planning must be done in several stages:

Long-range planning is the first stage. In this type of planning, the committee determines what they expect to be accomplished through the library ministry in the next five years. The objectives of the library would be laid before the committee in order that goals could be set that would achieve or improve the performance of the objectives. Programs would be sketched out that would result in the attainment of those goals.

Chapter 2 listed library goals. As you read them, you will see that resource materials, how-to books, and audiovisuals are needed to fulfill certain objectives. Plans must be formulated to implement the acquisition of such materials. Where will reaching the homes of the church families fit in? How will you improve your support of the curriculums used throughout the church? What will be your plans for teaching people how to use the tools of the library?

You will begin with those things you rate high on your priority list. Then year by year you will add on other needs, programs. How much money will be needed in five years? What changes will need to be made in the housing and organization?

Yearly planning. It is one thing to set your sights on what you expect to be in five years, but what will be done this year that will contribute to the reaching of the five-year goals? What materials will be added in this current year? What will the promotional program be to support your activities? How can the room be improved this year?

Monthly planning. Each month should have a special emphasis for promotion and development which ties into the yearly and ultimately the five-year plan. A workers' schedule should be prepared three weeks before the month begins. Promotional programs should be prepared at least one month ahead.

Weekly planning. Just as a Sunday School teacher should have a lesson plan for her class, so the librarian should have a weekly plan developed to begin with Sunday morning. Included in it should be:

The responsibility for each activity during the week; the special thrust to be made and how it will be executed; the meetings that must be attended; the promotional efforts that are to be made; the reports that are to be completed for church information.

4
Finances

It costs to begin and maintain a library. Most people do not realize the amount of money it takes to operate a church library. Often the church leadership gives the go-ahead and feels that somehow the finances will come together. Money is needed to acquire materials, to service materials, to promote materials and to purchase them.

Dedicated library workers give hundreds, sometimes thousands of dollars a year in their investment of time and money.

Compare what is being done in the public library with what is being done in the church library, and you will find something like this. In 1956, the cost of achieving a minimum standard of library service in a typical city of 100,000 was $3.00 per capita. In a city of 50,000, it was $3.40 per capita.

Take a church with a membership of 100 which might mean about 150 people in the church and its organizations. If $3.00 were allotted for each person, the amount would be about $450 per year. Yet, in the typical budget today, about twice that much is needed to do an average job in the library.

General material costs. To get a picture of the finances needed for a library, the following general figures are used to make it easy to follow. These are *average* costs at the time of writing. Some books cost more, some less: paperback books, $3.00 each; hardback books, $7.00 each;

flannelgraphs, $3.00 each; filmstrips, $9.00 each; cassette tapes (prerecorded) $7.00 each.

Starting a library. The cost of starting a library depends on the quantity of materials with which you want to begin. For example, an initial amount of $2500 would enable a library to start with approximately:

50 hardback books @ $7.00 each	=	$ 350.00
260 paperback books @ $3.00 each	=	780.00
Equipment	=	700.00
Supplies	=	170.00
AV hardware and software	=	500.00
Starting total		$2500.00

These figures are given only as an example of how to figure material costs. With rising manufacturing costs, book prices will average more than shown. Various amounts of equipment can be installed depending on whether you buy or have equipment made by carpenters in your church. Supplies will vary according to the circulation of materials. If your library is selecting only books, then the audiovisual amount will not be needed.

Monthly operating costs.

Cost of acquiring materials

Paperback books (10 per month @ $3.00 each)	=	$30.00
Hardback books (2 per month @ $7.00 each)	=	14.00
Audiovisuals	=	15.00
Supplies	=	6.00
Monthly acquisition totals		$65.00

Cost of servicing materials

Postage supplies	=	5.00
Library supplies	=	5.00
Equipment	=	10.00
Monthly service totals		$20.00

Cost of promotion materials

Supplies	=	$10.00
Grand total needed per month for operation		$95.00

Again, the above figures are given as examples of minimum operating costs.

Printed media will advance in price as will audiovisuals. The purchase of *audiovisuals* should be carefully thought out before spending money.

Part of the money may be budgeted for hardware and part for software. A determination must be made of the basic amount to spend for audiovisuals, and begin to buy according to that figure.

Postage money is needed because of the expense in writing letters and sending cards. Library *supplies* include date due slips, book pockets, book cards, etc. You may not spend the equipment amount each month, but accumulate enough to buy a needed piece. *Promotion* expenses include mimeo, postage and display supplies.

Establish a budget. Write out a monthly estimated goal for the items shown under the monthly operation costs.

That is, determine how many books and audiovisuals the library would like to acquire each month, and what they will cost. Some months, such as during summer, will have few or no acquisitions. Other months, they could run very high because of the type of promotion to be made. Estimate also the amount of money needed for supplies and equipment each month.

The total of all the costs per month will give an idea of how much money will be needed by the library. This figure will present a challenge as to how that money can be obtained. The monthly figures also will help to guard against overspending.

If the above information is taken to the church treasurer, he will be able to help set up a budget which will show: the expenditure items; the monthly cost of the items; estimated income for the month; actual income for the month; amount spent below or over the estimated income.

At the end of the year, the library will be able to present its financial statement to the church as do the other organizations; give quantities acquired and cost; give cost of supplies, services and promotion.

All of this will show the leadership and membership of the church that the library is being handled properly and efficiently as far as finances are concerned.

Planning to Raise Money

All kinds of schemes can be devised for raising money for the library. However, the best plan is God's plan—His people giving systematically to meet the needs of the church as God has led them. The library should be a part of the needs of the church, being met by the people of the church.

Motivation for giving. People need to know why it is important that a library ministry be started and maintained as a part of the church ministry. The objectives that have been formulated will help in presenting the importance of the library ministry. The people must also be made aware of what it costs for supplies, promotion, equipment and outreach.

Preparation for giving must include definite prayer. Ask God to touch the hearts of people to give.

Plan a budget. In preparation for each new church fiscal year, the library committee should prepare a budget to be presented to the church board and the members of the church at the annual business meeting. The budget might be considered a program for the coming year's activities with price tags attached to the various activities.

In presenting the budget, the librury does not only ask for a sum of money; it also explains what it expects to do with the money, why the activities are worth doing and how they fit into the total library picture and the church's needs.

(See in chapter 3, The Library Committee, p. 46.)

Promote. Plan the kind of presentations of the ministry you want to make. Chapter 10 will give you ideas for promotion.

Give service. Service will bring support. You cannot expect the church and individuals in the church to support the library unless it is being of service to them. People give to the general fund of the church if the ministry of the church is affecting their lives and those of others. People will give to the library ministry if it is affecting them; as they see people being helped by it; and as they see God using it.

Cautions in fund raising include the following: Don't become a beggar organization. Too many gimmicks or begging can cheapen the ministry.

Don't do your own thing without consideration of others. Monetary gifts to the library should not take away from what is being given to the church to help meet its financial obligations.

Don't fail to give a proper accounting of what is being done with the monies received.

Don't get lax in acknowledging the gifts that have been given.

Help people to give. Help them see their need for supporting the library. Help people to save money if it is only nickels, dimes and quarters through small banks that can be taken home and returned as soon as possible. Also a large bank constructed of posterboard and made like a book can be put on a library table to receive gifts—large or small.

Help people to direct their money to the library through the use of the regular church envelopes. When these envelopes are printed, the library should be listed as a possible designation for giving. If this is not possible, provide people with a special library envelope.

Have one or two outstanding library days a year. On these days the people of the church can hear about the library, can be urged to come into the library, can see displays of library materials, and can have the opportunity to add material to the library.

Library responsibility in giving. Let the congregation know of gifts to the library unless the donor requests otherwise. Provide donor plaques for gifts of equipment such as tables, bookshelves, cabinets, etc. Keep a permanent record of all gifts and memorials.

Regular Monetary Appropriations

From what sources can a church library expect to receive money?

The church budget. The library should be included as a monthly expense in the budget of the church. A minimum monthly figure for a church of 150 to 200 would be about $25. Why should a church board include the library in its budget?

The library is a part of the total church ministry and is important to the overall teaching ministry of the church. It is a valuable entity of the church. Material in the library can lead to the spiritual growth of the members. Money can be saved through the use of the same material by many people.

The Sunday School budget. A minimum monthly figure to be considered by the Sunday School to help in the operation of the library is $15. Why should the Sunday School include the library in its regular annual budget?

The library provides materials that support the curriculums being taught. Teachers can receive help for their class ministry. Their Bible background can be enriched. Their ability to teach can be sharpened. Supplementary materials can enhance their teaching. Library materials are important to the teacher training program. Students can find resource material in the library.

Organizational budgets. All groups in the church should be considered as potential sources of money. Possibly about $50 per month could be realized through budgeted monetary gifts from various organizations. Why should a church group help the library?

The use of library materials can help give meaning to the home life of young adults attending a Sunday School class. It can help mature adults with child or teen relationships. As a Junior class helps the library, new books can be provided for their reading as well as other juniors who will be coming along. All students can be helped in understanding the Bible better. Women's groups can help provide material especially geared to women's needs; the same for men.

Special Monetary Appropriations

Individual gifts. Provided the church board has been consulted and agreed, individuals in the church should be encouraged to give to the church library. Monies could be received in different ways such as:

Designation on church offering envelope—probably the best, most consistent method; use of special library envelopes; box on library table for coins to be given.

Pledged giving. Fifty people giving $1 a month equals $600 a year. Fifty people giving $5 two times a year equals $500.

Family giving. Encourage families to give. Help them to save their change. One family giving $5 per month for six months equals $30.

Birthday giving. Where a birthday offering is not received for missions, such an offering might be instituted as gifts for the library.

Selling Books

For profit

In considering the matter of a church or its library selling books for profit, some important factors must be taken into consideration:

It becomes a small business. If there is a book table in the church which sells materials for more than it pays for them, and for which the library or any other organization or person is responsible, it is subject to state laws.

This may require a tax number and license. Sales tax may have to be collected, reported and paid.

It could eventually affect the tax-free status of the church. The government frowns on mixing profit and non-profit operations.

The better way. Have your local Christian bookstore set up the book-table manned by your personnel. This way, they are the sellers and as such collect the tax money. In addition they can keep the current inventory coming into the table without a lot of work by library personnel.

Not for profit

Here are some ways libraries have found it profitable to promote the sale of non-profit books:

Book fair. Once a year the library contacts the local Christian bookstore and asks for books on consignment. It is best for the library committee to choose the books wanted, but bookstore personnel will always be glad to give suggestions to those making the choices. Place the books on a manned table and promote the purchase of them by the people of the church for the purpose of increasing the inventory of the library.

A procedure something like this could be set up: an individual chooses a book; he completes a card indicating if and what he would like on a book plate; the card and book are given to the attendant; the book is processed and becomes part of the library; the book is loaned first to the purchaser for the regular loan period.

Book shower. Prepare a list of books needed. Have a special table with the books and cards on which to put a name. The card would read, "For my church library from . . . ." Using a rubber band to join the book and card together, they are then placed in a decorated basket as a gift to the library.

Conference extension table. Whenever the church has a conference, have a table with books, cassettes and even visuals especially on the topic of the conference. Promote the fact that the conference can have lasting effects by individuals contributing to the purchase of an entire item or some contributing whatever they can. These materials can be used not only by them, but also by others in the future. The library collection can add materials on missions, evangelism, the home, etc., during these conferences.

Special Materials Appropriations

Not only do gifts of money help the library, but also gifts represented by books and audiovisuals help build a good collection.

Some ways materials can be given are through:

Memorial books. These are books given in recognition of one who has died. The choice of title for such books should be in collaboration with the one who is providing the money. Such a memorial should never lose its identity. This is protected through the use of a bookplate in the book as well as a record in the accession book or gift record file.

Living memorial books. Sometimes these books are called honor books or appreciation books. They are given at the time of the birth of a child; the birthday of a son or daughter; honoring a teacher who has done a commendable job; grandparents honoring a grandchild; a church member on his birthday, by the church; parents' recognition day.

For Mother's Day and Father's Day, provide a display of books from which children of any age can choose books their parents would like to read. Bookplates are provided to indicate that the books have been placed in the library to honor the parents. After the books are processed, they are given to the child to present to the parents to read and then return to the library.

Wanted books. Provide a "want list" showing books that are needed. Have a place where an individual can sign that he will provide a certain book.

Unwanted books. Often members of the congregation will have books lying around their home, no longer in use. If they are willing to part with the books, accept them on a selective basis only.

Pastor's concern books. Ask the pastor to channel special gifts to the library whenever possible. Provide him with a list of books needed in the next six months.

Bookstore plans. Check with your local Christian bookstore to see if they have a special plan for libraries that will enable you to get books without cost or at a lower cost.

(See in chapter 6, Purchase the Book Selected, p. 89.)

Library exchange. When you have duplicate books or books that have not been used for some time, consider trading them with another church library.

Consigned books. At special times, get books from your local Christian bookstore on consignment to display or use in non-profit sale of books.

Loan books. Check with church members and pastoral staff to see if they have any books they would be interested in loaning to the library for a limited period. Special care should be taken to identify these books and yet not mark them as other books would be marked.

Preservation of books:

A book saved from a short life makes more money available to buy current books for the library. Replacing lost or damaged books takes money from the current book fund. Take steps to protect every book properly.

When entering a new book into the library, cover the hardbacks with a plastic cover and strengthen the paperbacks. (See in chapter 6, Prepare the Book for Use, p. 93.)

Provide plastic covers (bags) for books when there is inclement weather that would affect the books.

Be sure every book is checked out properly.

Keep track of materials. By charging a fine for overdue books, you double your return. You receive the fine money plus you don't have to pay money out to replace the book.

Training personnel to use audiovisual equipment will prevent costly damage to both hardware and software.

5
Housing and Equipment

Many variables appear when housing and equipment are considered. Every church property layout is different. The space allotted to libraries has many dimensions. Needs for library services vary from one church to another. For this reason, general principles and ideas are given to act as guidelines.

The amount of equipment a library has or should have is dependent on available finances, space that is available, and the desire of the staff to develop the library. Some equipment must be purchased outright. Much equipment can be constructed by those in the church who are able to do carpenter work.

Library Locations

Library locations are classified under seven categories, in somewhat of a progression. Hopefully, if your library is in a very limited space situation, you will be able to improve on the dimensions in the near future.

If the location of your library discourages people from coming, work and pray for a location which makes it easier for people to take advantage of your services. If the space you have is not suitable for an efficient library operation, start now and work for a space that will solve this problem.

Portable Bookcase Library

The word "portable" indicates that this library has no permanent home. It is for the church that: (a) is very small; (b) has not caught the vision of the importance of the library; (c) just cannot find a permanent home for the library in the present church housing situation; (d) or cannot or will not properly support a library financially. This type of location is better than no location at all, but should be considered only a temporary situation.

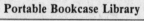

Portable Bookcase Library

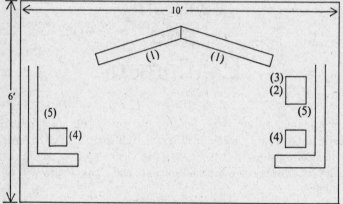

(1) Portable bookcase
(2) Card catalog
(3) Table for card catalog
(4) Folding chairs
(5) Portable partition

Where may such space be found?

In the narthex of the church; in a Sunday School department room; in a social room. *Minimum space needed* is 60 to 100 square feet.

Basic equipment includes the following:

• *Bookcases.* A pair of type 6 with back panels either three feet or six feet high. The bookcases should be hinged together. A pair of regular casters and a pair of brake casters under each case will make it easy to open, keep open or close them. Add a hasp and padlock to keep materials secured when the library is not open.

• *Card catalog cabinet*. A tray with a capacity of 1300 cards is needed for every 325 books. A cabinet type 1 or 2 can be used. A place to set the cabinet is needed such as a small table type 1, 36 inches × 36 inches.

• *Folding chairs*. Two would be very useful. One chair could be used for the staff member on duty. (This type of library should always be staffed when open.) The other chair could be available for patrons to use while consulting with the staff member or perusing a book.

• *Lap board*. Made of 5/8" plywood, 24" × 36". The staff member could use the board when writing or checking out a book. A small cardboard box could be stapled to the board to hold book cards, pencils, etc. Sometimes a leaf can be hinged to one of the bookcase shelves, and that would be even better.

• *Partition*. A pair of small portable partitions as shown in figure A could be used to set off the library, as it were, from the rest of the area where it is used.

• *Carpet*. A piece of indoor-outdoor carpet cut to fit the area would add much to the allotted space if the area is not already carpeted.

To open the library for service: open the bookcase to about 130° angle; put the rug down; set the partitions in place; position the chairs. Now the library is ready for people to make use of the materials.

Disadvantages: the capacity of the library will be limited, the types of media that can be handled are very restricted; the area could become so congested that it would be hard for individuals to get to the area and look at the materials.

Advantages: a church can get started with a library ministry; costs are minimal; the library can be located in the line of traffic; the library can be locked when not in use.

Making the most of the situation: paint or stain the equipment to complement the surrounding area; keep the library area and bookshelves clean and neat; dress up the area with flowers, special displays, posters; keep regular hours just as if the library was in its own room; don't disturb other people in the area with loud talking.

Keep books with possibilities of moving fast on the shelves. Other books could be kept in a storage area if shelf space becomes short.

However, all books should be listed in the card catalog.

Don't let the people of the church get the idea that this is a permanent arrangement. Promote a better location. A poster may be used to show a diagram of the library room you need. Title it, "Our Next Step." Convey the fact that the library ministry is an important one and needs its own room. Ask the people to pray about it. Work with the church board to get the room you need.

Services that can be provided: with a pair of type 1 bookcases, up to 30 hardback and 1,000 paperback books could be made available for loan; with a pair of type 3 bookcases, up to 20 hardback and 400 paperback books could be stored.

Share-a-room Library

As the name implies, the library is forced to share a room with another church ministry. Hopefully this too is a temporary situation until a special room can be found in which to house the library.

Where might this type of space be found? In a Sunday School class-

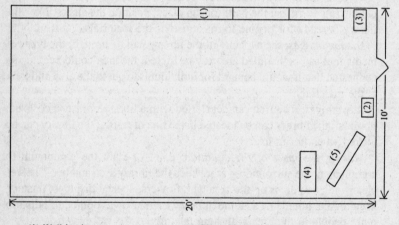

Share-a-room Library

(1) Wall bookcases
(2) Card catalog
(3) Storage cabinet
(4) File cabinet
(5) Service desk; if a service desk is a problem, make one wall bookcase.

room; in a room used by another Christian education organization; in the choir room, social room or overflow room.

Minimum space needed: would be about 12 feet of clear wall space plus room for necessary equipment.

Basic equipment would include: bookcases—enough type 1 to cover the wall space allotted. If a table or desk cannot be fitted into the room, substitute one type 5 bookcase. Card catalog cabinet (one type 2); storage cabinet (one type 1, 36 inches high, for supplies, audiovisual hardware and software; file cabinet (one type 3, four drawer); service desk (one desk type 1 or table type 1).

Disadvantages: the room may not be available to use during the Sunday School hour; if students come to class early or teachers go over their time, part of the library time will be lost; a proper library decor or atmosphere may not be developed because of traffic, chairs and class equipment; perhaps the room cannot be locked. It would always be exposed to people without supervision when used by the other organization.

Advantages: the library is in a room; more shelf space will be available than if a portable library were used; there would be room for some equipment which could not be used in a portable library situation.

Making the most of the situation: work out a definite time schedule with the other organization that uses the room; spend time considering how you can utilize the space allotted to the library to the best advantage; place a library sign on or by the door with hours of operation.

Use directional signs on the church campus to help people find the room in which the library is being housed. If the room needs cleaning or painting, work with those in the other organization and the church board to accomplish this.

Perhaps if a class is using the room, its members might help raise the finances to carpet the room if it is not already carpeted. If the room has poor lighting, try to get this improved. Keep the library area neat. This is not only for the sake of those using the library, but also for those with whom the room is shared.

Have an understanding with organizational members that they will not take materials off the shelves unless a member of the library staff is present.

Ask for time to speak to the other occupants of the room to tell them what a privilege they have in sharing their room with such an important church function.

Services that can be provided:

With three type 1 bookcases, 45 hardbacks and 1,500 paperbacks could be made available for circulation.

With one type B1 storage cabinet, 50 filmstrips and 200 cassette tapes along with a projector and a tape player could be stored.

With a file cabinet type C1, a vertical file could be begun and up to 10 flannelgraphs stored.

Mini-room Library

In library workshops, many times reports are made by librarians that their library is in a cubby hole, closet or some other tiny room. Sometimes these "rooms" are so small it is difficult to turn around in them.

Where are these rooms found? in an area too small for a classroom; in an unused storage room; in a small area of a room that has been partitioned off.

Minimum space needed: if the area allocated is smaller than 80 square feet, it may not be worth moving into. Even a room of 150 square feet could be classified as a mini-room.

Basic equipment would include: bookcases (enough type 1 to cover two of the four walls). To take advantage of every bit of space, use a type 2 bookcase above the file and storage cabinet. Card catalog cabinet (one or two type 2 cabinets). Storage cabinet (one type 2). Service desk (one desk type 1 or table type 1).

Disadvantages: There is not much room to move around. A crowded look is not an inviting look. The amount of materials is limited. There could be ventilation problems. There would be no place for people to sit and examine or use the materials.

Advantages: It is entirely a library situation. The librarian has the option to set the room up any way she sees fit. The room can be used when it is needed. The room can be locked when not in use.

Making the most of the situation: Paint the wall and ceiling a light color to give the effect of a larger area. Have good lighting so the room is bright. Put a carpet on the floor. Perhaps a portable service desk could be

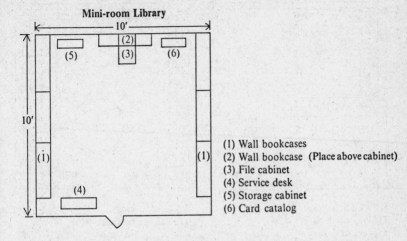

Mini-room Library

(1) Wall bookcases
(2) Wall bookcase (Place above cabinet)
(3) File cabinet
(4) Service desk
(5) Storage cabinet
(6) Card catalog

put just outside the library when it is in operation to allow as much room as possible for people to move about. A library housed in a small room with proper administration can be as effective as a library with a larger room, not properly administered.

Services that can be provided: with four type M bookcases and one type A4 bookcase, 60 hardbacks and 2,000 paperbacks can be stored. With a storage cabinet type B1, about 50 filmstrips and a projector and about 100 cassette tapes and a player can be made available to the people of the church.

With a type C1 file *cabinet*, a vertical file can be developed; 10 flannelgraphs and about 50 transparencies (without frames) can be stored.

Dual-room Library

Here, two distinctly separate rooms, often not directly connected, are used for the overall library operation. The reason for two rooms is that the room provided for the library services is just not adequate for the church program and one larger room is not available. This does not mean there are two libraries, but that one library is functioning in two places.

Some ways in which two rooms could be utilized are: children's

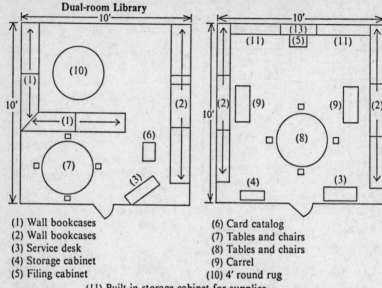

Dual-room Library

(1) Wall bookcases
(2) Wall bookcases
(3) Service desk
(4) Storage cabinet
(5) Filing cabinet
(6) Card catalog
(7) Tables and chairs
(8) Tables and chairs
(9) Carrel
(10) 4' round rug
(11) Built-in storage cabinet for supplies

materials in one room; youth and adult materials in the other. Books in one room; audiovisuals in the other. Storage of materials in one room; display, study tables, story rug, carrel in the other.

Where might such rooms be found? Almost anywhere on the church campus that lends itself to this type of layout. The ideal situation is to have the rooms adjacent to each other or across the hallway from each other. They could be in the same building or two different buildings if absolutely necessary.

Minimum space needed: the minimum area would be from 100 to 200 square feet in each room, depending on the use of the room.

Basic equipment should include: bookcases (for a preschool area: one or two type 4 bookcases; type 1 book rack; for a grade school area: one or two type 2 bookcases; for a teen and adult area: two or three type 1 bookcases). Card catalog cabinet (one type 2, four-drawer cabinet). Storage cabinet (one type 1, 72 inches high). Service desk (one type 1 desk). Special cabinet (one type 1 for flat graphics).

Table and chairs—for a children's study area (type 1 or 2, 24 inches high); for an adult study area (type 1 or 2, 29 inches high). *Carrel* (if there is room for a private study area of any media, a carrel type 1). *Story rug* (to be used in the preschool area).

Disadvantages: it is more difficult to control two areas than one; it requires more helpers; the catalog might have to be split.

Advantages: there can be flexibility in the use of the rooms; two rooms are better than one small room; it could increase the overall service effectiveness of the library through specialized areas.

Making the most of the situation: Use different color schemes in each room. Use a two-part sign on the door of each room. Indicate on one side what functions of the library are in that room. On the other side, indicate the functions of the other room and where it can be found. A monthly workers' meeting is important to let the entire staff know what is going on in each room.

Services that can be provided: with two type A6 bookcases; two type A3 bookcases; and two type A1 bookcases, 70 hardbacks and 1,400 paperbacks can be stored. With a type B2 cabinet, about 100 filmstrips and a projector; about 200 cassette tapes and a player; an overhead projector can be stored. With a type C2 file cabinet, a vertical file; store up to 50 flannelgraphs and 100 transparencies.

Central-satellite Library

This library is composed of a main room located in the best possible

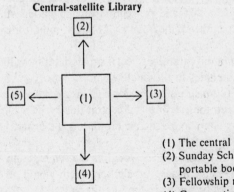

Central-satellite Library

(1) The central library
(2) Sunday School Department room
    portable bookcase
(3) Fellowship room—wall bookcase
(4) Congregating area—freestanding bookcase
(5) Front door ministry—book cart

location. In addition, the library would operate just as many satellite libraries in various locations on the church property as the library staff could personally handle. No satellite library should be left unstaffed.

The difference between this type of a library and the dual-room library is that the satellite library would be in rooms used by other organizations with materials especially selected from the central library for the use of the people in that particular organization.

On the other hand, the rooms of the dual-room library would contain all the materials of the library. The principle of the satellite library is that if people will not come into the library room, the library should go to them. They can be placed wherever people congregate.

Where can space be found? In a Sunday School department room; in a fellowship room; in a small chapel used during the week; in the narthex of the church; near a drinking fountain; outside the front door of the church.

Basic equipment: the central library would use the same equipment as found in the other rooms described depending on its size. Examples of equipment that could be used for satellite libraries are the same as they would be in area situations given under dual-room library.

Disadvantages: a larger staff is needed; extra work is required to keep all satellites functioning effectively; definite planning is needed to provide a good selection in each area week by week.

Advantages: the satellite libraries are where the people are. All materials have a home in the central library. This provides for proper follow-up of materials; control of selection and prevention of duplication of materials. The presence of a member of the library staff helps promote the library as a whole.

Making the most of the situation: carefully select the materials that will best help the individual who comes to the satellite library.

Appoint someone to take full responsibilities for checking out books, and to act as a liaison between the satellite and central library.

Provide identifying library signs for each area promoting the central/satellite concept.

Services that can be provided: the services would be the same as any other library type with comparable space. In addition, there would be better motivational experiences for those in the satellite areas.

Outerspace Library

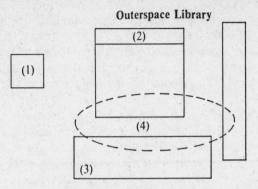

(1) A building away from the mainstream of traffic
(2) A room very difficult to get to
(3) A room in a far-off corner
(4) Main area of traffic

Outerspace Library

This term is used because this type of library is so far away from the flow of traffic. Sometimes one wonders if it can ever be found by anyone except the faithful few.

Where is it usually found? In a direction that people would not normally go. For example: under the choir loft, in a far corner of the church basement, in a not-too-frequented area of the church property, in a building adjacent to the church property.

Minimum space should not be less than those mentioned for the mini-room library. However, one would hope that with the distance problem, much more space might be allotted. To have both space and distance problems would make it very difficult to operate.

Depending on the size of the area allotted, basic equipment should be as described in other library types.

Disadvantages: it is difficult to get people to think about the library especially when the room cannot be seen—"out of sight, out of mind." Much more promotion has to be done in order to compensate for the location.

It is difficult to get people to take the time to find the library even if they know about it. It does not give the appearance of the library being a vital part of the church program.

Advantages: the room would be solely for the library ministry. The room could be developed to the most efficient use by the staff. More space could be provided for serving than if a mini-room were given closer to church activities.

Making the most of the situation: work for an "unusual" room to interest people in coming to see and use the materials. Increase the amount of promotion. Use directional signs. Work in cooperation with the teachers for planned visits to the library. Have a quality library that meets the needs of organizations as well as individuals. Use satellite libraries.

Services that can be provided: depending on the space you have and the equipment involved, the same services from the mini-library to the ideal library can be provided.

Ideal Library
This is the kind of library that has housing and equipment which meets the needs of the teaching and learning ministries of the church.

Where can such space be found? An ideal library could be placed in one of several locations depending on the layout of the church property. General principles for an excellent location are:

Where the majority of the people can *see* the library as they move about the church property. Where the library is able to *serve* the Christian education organizations effectively and efficiently. Where the library can be *used* throughout the week no matter where the center of gathering is located.

Minimum space needed is dependent on the size of your church. The larger the church, the more possibilities for the ministry of the library and the greater need for more space. If the Sunday School enrollment is taken as a basis of computing the amount of space needed, these minimum amounts are suggested:

Sunday School enrollment: 100 or less—at least 150 square feet; 200-300, at least 250 square feet; 300-500, at least 500 square feet; 1,000 or more, at least 800 square feet.

To determine basic equipment needs, make a scale layout of your area.

Ideal Library—showing suggestions for various areas of the library

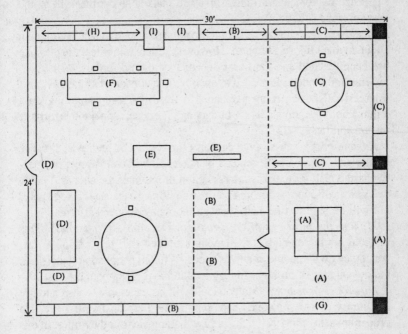

(A) Audiovisual area—carrels; built-in cabinets
    along walls for equipment storage
(B) Book storage area—wall shelving;
    freestanding stacks
(C) Children's area—wall shelving; reading table, chairs
(D) Patron's service area—checkout desk; catalog; door
(E) Display area—table for displays; double-faced bulletin board
(F) Study area—study tables and chairs
(G) Work area—work desk
(H) Reference area
(I) Other printed media area—file cabinet for vertical file; magazine rack

List the equipment you would like in your library. Refer to the pages of suggested equipment for dimensions and make a layout that will be the best for your situation.

Disadvantages: it may be hard to imagine that anyone would complain about an ideal library situation. However, people might feel the ultimate has been reached and the library needs to grow no further.

Time and money are needed to operate. Just as a larger church requires a larger budget and more personnel to fulfill its responsibilities, so a larger library requires a larger budget and more personnel to perform its responsibilities.

Advantages: larger storage capacity for books and audiovisuals. The library can offer learning center advantages. It will be in proper perspective to the rest of the Christian education program of the church. People will not be discouraged from entering the library because it is too small, but will be able to find help through the many services afforded.

Making the most out of the situation. Develop a proper staff. This includes having enough staff, having a trained staff and having a staff concerned about people and their needs. Without people doing their job, the advantages of an ideal library location and equipment are lost.

Do proper promotion. Many people will not take time to visit and use the library unless someone keeps reminding them of the privilege. Do proper housekeeping. Keep the library looking clean and inviting. In this way, the library says, "We are a going and growing organization." Good housekeeping never stops.

Services that can be provided. With ideal housing, sufficient equipment and a properly trained staff, a church library should have many opportunities for serving God's people. Many of these opportunities are recorded throughout the pages of this book.

Cooperative Church Libraries

Church libraries could add to their effectiveness if libraries serving churches of like faith would work together and make their material available to the members of all the cooperating churches.

Especially in larger suburban areas where people can travel easily, public libraries cooperate in sharing their loaning materials. The local

Cooperative Libraries

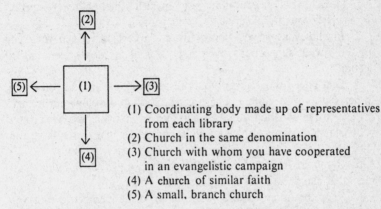

(1) Coordinating body made up of representatives from each library
(2) Church in the same denomination
(3) Church with whom you have cooperated in an evangelistic campaign
(4) A church of similar faith
(5) A small, branch church

library issues a card which may be used at a number of other libraries in an area inter-library plan. Each of the cooperating libraries probably has a little different emphasis in selection and so some will have materials that the other libraries do not feel will move for them.

Church librarians in a given locality could do the same thing. They could join together to make their materials available to the people of the cooperating churches. Then a member of one church could be free to call the other librarians with the idea of borrowing some book not found in his own.

For such an arrangement to work, each library should:

Issue library cards (See in chapter 3, Operating Policies, p. 48.); be open at times other than when the regular services of the churches are in progress; have quarterly meetings that would bring together the library staffs to coordinate their activities, publicity and ideas for the future; make telephone numbers of librarians available for card holders to make inquiries.

Such an arrangement could give the people of your church an opportunity to have a good many more materials at their disposal. Larger libraries could be of real service to smaller libraries. The cooperating churches could be the churches of your denomination or those with whom you would normally cooperate in a city-wide meeting, etc.

Principles of Location

1. In whatever type your library fits, make it a quality library—quality in materials, quality in service to your people.

2. In whatever type your library fits, do the best job you can where you are. Follow the suggestions given in the *Making the most of the situation* section.

3. Don't get discouraged if your present location is not all you want it to be. With vision, faith and hard work, you can develop your library.

4. Don't be satisfied with the status quo, even if you have what can be called an ideal library. If you do, your library effectiveness will begin to slip.

5. If you are in one of the smaller type libraries, buy or build equipment that can be used in other locations as you grow.

6. Keep the library before your church so the members will have a growing respect for it. Through promotion, tell what the library can do, the blessings people have recieved, materials available and circulation figures.

7. Build a staff that truly serves and is enthusiastic in its approach to the ministry.

8. Keep reaching out to where people are.

Basic Areas within the Library

Once space has been allocated to the library, then the space must be laid out for the best possible use. Some basic areas need to be kept in mind as you consider the layout of the library.

Book Storage Area

Part of the library space must be given over to storing books in such a way that they can be retrieved quickly by patrons when needed. Display is not important in this area although most church libraries must combine storage and display.

Equipment needed. Books need to be stored on shelves and not in boxes. When building shelves, keep these suggestions in mind:

Use adjustable shelving rather than fixed shelves which cannot be moved up or down. Brackets mounted on pegboard backings; standards using brackets fastened to a back panel; or standards fastened to the side of the upright boards with brackets will allow for adjustment.

Use standard size width of three feet.

Wall bookcases should be fastened to the wall to keep them from tipping and injuring someone.

Shelves can be colorful. They do not have to be a drab color. One color could be used throughout or colors could be mixed.

Some accessories that are needed to use with shelving are: shelf label holder; book supports; range label holders.

A formula for figuring the needed shelf space is: approximately 6 volumes of hardbacks per linear foot of shelving or 18 paperbacks per linear foot of shelving. Keep in mind that 90 percent of books are no more that 11 inches in height.

Location. The best place for an exclusive book storage area is toward the back of the library. If your space is adequate, use the "stacks" concept as found in the public library.

If you have an acute space problem, relatively slow circulating books could be put in a separate location which might be called the "archives." The shelving could be put in another room on the church property such as a classroom or storage room.

Shelving could also be constructed off the church property in someone's spare room or in a garage not easily accessible. The books would have to be "ordered" by the patron, using the card catalog.

Services that could be provided. While the book storage area is an accessible place for patrons to use freely, the audiovisual storage area should be in a security area. Audiovisual materials and equipment must be handled with great care or they can be permanently damaged by carelessness. Only library personnel should be permitted to release the software and hardware stored in the area. Patrons who wish to know what is available can refer to the card catalog for detailed information.

Equipment needed for audiovisual storage includes: storage cabinet; cassette storage cabinet; filmstrip storage cabinet, and special cabinet.

Location should be in a security area that can be locked.

Teachers need to be informed of what materials and equipment are in the area, motivated to use them, trained to use them, and if necessary helped to use them in class. If the service is not provided, two negative things can take place. (1) The materials could rot on the shelves or (2) the materials could be ruined in the classroom.

Patron's Service Area

Here people can be helped when coming into the library. In the public library, service is specialized and given in several locations, but in the average church library the services are usually performed in one area.

Equipment needed includes a service desk and a card catalog cabinet. Location should be near the main entrance.

Services that can be provided include the following:

• *Circulation assistance*—books and audiovisuals charged out and returned to the area. Library cards can be processed from here.

• *Reference assistance*—reference materials should be shelved in this area to set them off as non-circulating books.

• *Provide information*—answer questions, help meet needs, show how to use library tools.

• *Receive information*—find out the reaction of patrons to library services, books they have read. Receive their suggestions for materials to be put into the library.

Some library detail could be done here, but it would be better to do tasks like cataloging and making book repairs elsewhere.

(See in chapter 3, Clerical Workers, p. 41.)

Children's Area

A special effort should be made by library personnel to help children. An area that is adaptable to their size and needs will encourage them to use the library. Equipment needed in this particular area includes bookcases; a story rug; tables and chairs.

An ideal location would be in a corner where low bookcases could be used to separate the area from the rest of the library.

Services that could be provided. This area could be used not only as a place to display books for children to choose and take out, but a place to read books in the library or to have someone read to them during a story hour.

(See in chapter 12, Developing Readers to Enjoy the Ministry, p. 170.)

Study Area

If you have sufficient room in the library, the library can become a learning center where people can come in, take books off the shelf, sit down and read for pleasure in quietness, search for resources, continue study or view audiovisual materials. This area would be more for older children, teens and adults.

Equipment needed includes the following: table and chairs; carrel.

Services that can be provided. Help patrons with research work; help teachers use audiovisuals with their lessons; provide a quiet place for study.

Display Area

This is a motivational area. Fifty books on a shelf with only the spines showing is not much of an incentive for anyone to read or search out books on a particular subject. In the display area, books and audiovisuals are isolated to show them individually or as related to other items on a certain subject.

Equipment needed for the display area includes a small table; top of storage cabinet; top of file cabinet; top of a bookcase.

Location of the display area should be near the main entrance of the library.

Services that can be provided. Show the new books recently received. Emphasize books on special topics. Give ideas as to what is in the library. Display books correlated with the pastor's message or adult class lessons.

(See in chapter 10, Purposes of Promotion, p. 135.)

Work Area

This is a place where staff workers can take care of library details.

Equipment needed is a good-size worktable.

If possible, locate this area outside the library or behind a partition if it must be in the library room.

Services that can be provided. Book and audiovisual repairs; book and audiovisual cataloging.

Decor of the Room

How does the room you now have look? Can you evaluate it from the standpoint of a visitor coming into the library? If not, ask someone who can be objective to do it for you. The decor and features can make people feel welcome or make them feel they should leave as soon as possible.

The atmosphere of the library should be that of a gracious home living room.

The color scheme used can make or destroy the atmosphere desired. Different colors on different walls of the room can give the effect of a larger room. Some say bright colors stimulate people to study. Others say quieter colors are more suitable for a library.

Trophies, flowers, curios and pictures also can add to the decor. Rate your library on cleanliness, neatness, brightness, distinctiveness, friendliness, attentiveness, action, patrons' mental feeling.

Look up. Is the *ceiling* clean, bright, reflective? Is it acoustically absorbing to help deaden noise? Look down. Is the *floor* vibrant? Is it carpeted to give aesthetic warmth to the room?

Is there a need for general *lighting* to give life to the room? This will help people to see the book titles clearly and to scan a book. A lamp at the reading table will help with close reading.

Does it get stuffy in the room? Can you warm the room when necessary or cool it when necessary? Is the *ventilation* good?

It is important to have an inviting *entrance*. Would it help to paint the door? Is the door easy to open for both children and adults? In these days when the world is doing much for the handicapped, what about your library? Do you have a ramp and door size for a wheelchair?

Is there a lock on the door? A lock is not only to protect against stealing form outsiders, but it keeps people from removing books from the library without a correct record being made. Library records must show where each piece of material is and when it will be returned if it has been loaned. Many extra dollars as well as hours of work are spent each year by libraries just to track down and replace materials that have been forgotten by people who did not make a proper check-out record.

6
Flow
of
Work

What happens in a library when the decision is made to add a book to the collection? There are several things that must take place before any book is ready for circulation. This chapter will go over the various steps in the process.

In many libraries all of the steps must be done by the librarian with little help. However, by involving other people, there can be specialization, and as a result a better job will be done by each staff member.

The work in some areas should be undertaken only by trained library personnel. The work in other areas can be done by people who are able to follow directions and yet may know little about the technical aspects of processing books.

It pays to lay out a definite procedure to be used when entering a new book into the library. Laying such a foundation will be especially valuable as your library increases in activity. A lot of work is involved in this aspect of the library ministry. If it is done well, it will pay off in efficiency and effectiveness for years to come.

Select the Book

When determining who will select materials, the following questions must be answered:

Will the librarian have the sole responsibility? Will the responsibility be shared with the library committee? Will a special book committee be set up? Who will make the ultimate choice of books?

Someone must have the responsibility of material selection coordinator. It is an important responsibility to narrow the choice from thousands of books available to those relatively few books to be selected that will serve the church best.

Usually the librarian carries the responsibility of selector. For simplification, this person will be designated as the selector. In working with the library committee, organizational representatives and church leaders, the selector determines the specific titles to be ordered at any given time. (See in chapter 3, The Librarian, p. 38.)

To be an ideal selector, there are six things of which the selector should have a knowledge:

Book titles. A selector must be familiar with a great number of titles, not merely the titles on her library shelves. Book selection involves the consideration of far more titles than the selector actually buys. Knowing titles involves understanding what the titles are saying with regard to the subject or subjects covered in the book.

Sometimes a title does not reflect the true meaning of the book. Some titles are catch titles rather than descriptive titles. Knowing a number of titles on a given subject will enable a selector to weigh books one against the other and intelligently decide which book is the better one to buy at a given time.

Why is it necessary to have such a broad knowledge of titles? Suppose the selector determines there is a need for a book on the subject of prayer. With a limited knowledge, she may not be able to suggest the best book on prayer for the people of her church. But with book titles at her fingertips, she can begin to work toward locating the best book on the subject for her library. There will be other things to consider than the title, but this is a starting place.

Outstanding Christian authors. A selector should be able to tell who are the leading authors and what types of material they write.

Publishers of religious books. More and more publishers are coming into the Christian book market. The philosophies of their operations differ.

Costs. The price of a book should be looked at in relationship to the actual content of the book; the size of the book; the potential readership; the binding; the type of paper being used.

In other words, when the selector is about to buy a book, she should know what she is getting for her money.

Library inventory. Before making a final decision, the selector should check the card catalog to see if a copy of the book is already in the library, and how many comparable books there are in the library on the subject. If there are enough, it might be well to choose a book on another subject.

Good reason. An ideal selector will always have a good reason for her selections. Some of those reasons are:

It is a book *needed* by individuals in the church. The selector has sensed that a book on a certain subject would fill a spiritual need if read and appropriated.

It is a book *requested* by a number of people. It is not that the selector alone has become excited, or that one individual out of a hundred or more has asked for the book, but several people have talked about the book, or have come into the library asking for a book on the subject. If such is not the case, it might be better to borrow the book from another church library.

It is a book *recommended* by those who have purchased a copy or have read it. They feel it could be of help to others in the church.

It is a book *referred to* by a person in a place of leadership. Sometimes the pastor, a Sunday School teacher or a visiting speaker will speak highly of a book.

It is a book with a pertinent and *current subject*. It is a subject about which people are looking for information to answer questions they have.

Every book entered into the library whether purchased or received as a gift should have a "stamp" of qualification. That stamp is the prayerful and careful consideration of the book by a trained person.

(See in chapter 3, The Library Committee, p. 46.)

Purchase the Book Selected

Purchasing anything in the name of the church by an individual or organization, including the library, should be done by someone who knows the procedure practiced in the church. The person authorized to do the actual purchasing, called the buyer, should develop a good book-buying policy which would be efficient and systematically organized.

Such Policy Should Consider:

The time for buying. Will books be bought weekly, monthly, twice a year or just at random? It is better to schedule a time to buy rather than make a special trip to the Christian bookstore for every book.

A procedure for buying. First, prepare a 3″ x 5″ buying information card for each book. Record the title, author, publisher, price, and source of purchase. Show the order date. If for some reason the book had to be back ordered by the supplier and was not received within two weeks, the buyer could follow up to see what the situation was.

When the book is received, show the date received on the card. This should include an inspection of the book to see that it is in good condition. Then place the book in a section for cataloging.

Buying Information Card

```
┌─────────────────────────────────────────────────────────────┐
│                                                             │
│  Title _____ Price _____    │
│                                                             │
│  Author _____ │
│                                                             │
│  Publisher _____ │
│                                                             │
│  Source of purchase _____ │
│                                                             │
│  Date of purchase _____ Date received _____ │
│                                                             │
│  Follow-up information _____ │
│                                                             │
│  _____  │
│                                                             │
│  _____  │
│                                                             │
└─────────────────────────────────────────────────────────────┘
```

This card can also be used to list titles of books
which you may be interested in purchasing for the future.

Secondly, *authorize payment for the book*. The way authorization is given will depend on how the bills of the church are paid. Whoever pays the bills will want to be sure the merchandise has been received and is in good condition. If someone besides the buyer makes the payment, a written authorization should be given indicating that it is all right to make payment. Sometimes a verbal authorization can be misunderstood or forgotten.

A source for buying. In the overall picture, your local Christian bookstore can be the best place to buy materials. What are the advantages of patronizing your local Christian bookstore?

It has a *ministry* to the people of your community just as you do to your church. It is *easy to contact* by phone should a problem arise. It makes *no charge* for transportation which can be very costly. It has *current and past titles* on hand as well as a great variety of titles.

It has books from *many publishers*. Their personnel are happy to work with you on *special orders*. They will take care of any *defective copies* that may appear. The bookstore becomes a place of *training* for the library staff. It provides in-store *displays* of materials. It provides brochures, catalogs and other *promotional* materials from the publishers to help with the selection of materials and promotion.

Your local bookstore can provide a list of the *top selling* books, books for *special library promotions* and provide suggestions as to how to make your *library dollar* go farther. To sum it all up, it will give you *service*. Evaluate the bookstore from which you buy for service as well as charge.

An inventory record. The inventory record is a complete list not only of what is on the shelf, but also all that belongs there. For years, librarians of all kinds have used printed accession sheets on which to record every book entered into the library. Accession information includes: title, author, publisher, copyright date, cost and any remarks about the book such as where it was purchased or by whom it was given.

In recent years, shelf cards often have been substituted for the accession sheet. The advent of the unit card for books such as those issued by the Library of Congress has promoted the use of the shelf card. The shelf card may be a duplicate of the main entry card with the following information typed on the back: date of purchase, cost and source of purchase or donor.

The advantage of duplicating the main entry card is that if damage should come to the library and the card catalog, it would not be necessary to go through all the work involved in preparing the information for the books that would be replaced. Some libraries omit the notes, contents and tracings and list the additional information at the bottom of the card.

Either the accession record or the shelf cards, verified by a yearly inventory, make a good record for insurance purposes in case of damage to the library and its contents. The shelf card makes it more convenient to take an inventory as the cards are filed by the way the books are on the shelves.

Either record should be kept in a safe location away from the library. When the inventory record is made, the buying information card then can be destroyed.

Evaluate the Book to Be Entered

Before a book is actually purchased for the library, every precaution should be made to determine if the book will fit into your particular ministry. As the selector works with her committee, reads book reviews and talks with employees of a Christian bookstore, she can be pretty well assured that the book will (or will not) fit into the collection. However, there is only one way to determine the full value of the book to the library and that is by having someone read the book objectively.

One or more persons can be chosen to read books before they are prepared for use. These persons should enjoy reading, know what to look for when reading and be able tt evaluate what they have read. The information gleaned can be of help in promotion of the book and in verifying that the right kinds of books are in the library. It also can help the cataloger in her search of materials for the card catalog.

A book evaluator should be able to do these six things:

Write a short summary of the book. To be able to say in a few words what the important things are about a book is an art in itself. A poor summary might say nothing that would help people but actually would discourage them from reading the book. On the other hand, the summary could enable a person to get a good bird's-eye view of the book. It could be a means of motivating a person to read the book.

Give the main thrust of the book. Although there may be several books on the same subject in the library, the thrust of each book could be entirely different. By *thrust* is meant the purpose the author had in mind when writing; the way he expressed that purpose; the results he expected to be seen in the lives of the readers. Some books are purely academic and thought-provoking. Others are devotional, highly motivational and spirtually stimulating.

Interpret the doctrine of the book. Basically the books put into the library should support the doctrine of the church. If they do not, and are there for comparative purposes only, such books should be so designated.

Detect the Christian ethics reflected in the book. Ethics refers to the standards of conduct and moral judgment of individuals. Today with a change of standards of conduct by many, it is important to check each book to see if what is written agrees with the standards taught by the church.

Note the subjects included in the book. The more information that can be given about a book for potential readers, the more likely it will be to be read and the more valuable the book will be.

Make recommendations to the library committee. The evaluation could state why or why not the book should be put into the library. The evaluator could indicate who would enjoy the book the most—a serious reader, or one who likes lighter materials. She could also state for what age the book is written.

(See in chapter 3, Evaluators, p. 42.)

(See in chapter 3, Cataloger, p. 43.)

Prepare the Book for Use

Hardback Books

Most hardback books have attractive dust jackets which have great promotional value. A determination must be made as to what will be done with them. Here are some possibilities:

• Take the jacket off completely. Those who do this usually use the jackets for promotional purposes. The most likely place for them to be found is on the bulletin board in the library. They may or may not ever get back on the book.

• Cut off the flaps of the jacket and paste them in the book. The flaps contain pertinent information about the book and author. The rest of the jacket could be used for promotion.

• Leave the jacket on the book. This is the most effective use of the jacket. Publishers put thousands of dollars into jackets because they know jackets help sell the books. No greater promotion is possible than to display the book with its motivational cover.

The chances are far greater for an individual when seeing a book with a jacket to decide to borrow that book than if the jacket is in one place and the book in another. Even after the new books have been promoted in the new book display, they still will brighten the library room and promote the book when on the shelf.

If you decide to keep the dust jacket on the book, use a plastic cover to protect both cover and book. Without it, the jacket will soon become damaged and will be detrimental to the use of the book.

Paperback Books

The paperback can be put on the shelf in the same condition in which it is received. Or with a little work, the book can be protected for a much longer life.

Protect the covers with the use of a clear contact paper. Protect the spine with the use of a clear spine cover. Protect the binding with the use of a binding tape on the inside of the book. Have the paperback made into a hardback. Some companies specialize in this type of work.

Check all pages. Occasionally books come from printers with pages not fully cut. To let a patron cut them may be disastrous if he is not careful, resulting in ragged or torn pages.

Open the book properly. Hold the book on its spine on a flat surface. Open the front cover flat with the surface. Run your fingers along the seam. Next, open the back cover flat with the surface. Run your fingers along the seam.

Then, taking a few pages each time, alternate opening the pages from front to back, each time running your fingers along the seam. Do this until you come to the center of the book.

Opening each new book in this way will help the book to lie open without pressure. If this is not done, a patron may be upset because the book will not stay open easily and with one harsh bend will "break" the binding.

Clean the book if necessary. When a book is entered into the library, it should be in the best possible condition. Some of the used books received or books purchased as closeouts may be dirty. If the edges or some of the pages themselves are dirty, use an art-gum eraser to help remove some of the dust. If the book cover needs freshening up, try some spray cleaner.

Catalog the Book

The process of cataloging a book involves two phases. The first phase is called *subject cataloging*. In this phase, four steps are taken to arrive at a valid classification number and to assign a subject heading for the book.

Step 1: Examine the book for information that can be used as a basis for determining the classification number.

Step 2. Use the tools that are available to help place the book in the proper section of the library.

Step 3. Assign a valid classification number.

Step 4. Assign a subject heading for the book.

The second phase of cataloging is described as *descriptive cataloging*. In this phase, three basic steps apply.

Step 1. Gather as much information as possible about each book through reading the book and the recommendation of others.

Step 2. Choose the necessary information to describe the book in the catalog.

Step 3. Write this information on a work slip to be used to type the main and added entry cards.

(See in chapter 8, Classification, p. 111.)

Process the Book

Processing can be done by clerical workers who lack technical library skills. Several basic things are done.

Make necessary entries into the book. Enter the call number in pencil on the upper left-hand corner of the title page. Accession number (if used) should be entered in ink on the title page just above the name of the publisher.

Entries and Inserts into a Book

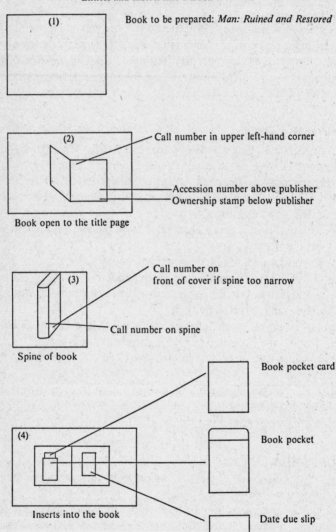

Book to be prepared: *Man: Ruined and Restored*

(2) Call number in upper left-hand corner

Accession number above publisher
Ownership stamp below publisher

Book open to the title page

(3) Call number on
front of cover if spine too narrow

Call number on spine

Spine of book

Book pocket card

(4) Book pocket

Inserts into the book

Date due slip

Library identification should be stamped in one or more places: across the top or bottom edges of the book while it is held closed; the bottom of the title page underneath the name of the publishers; on a special page which the librarian selects (same page for each book); on the bottom of the book pocket.

Spine inscription is important. Prepare a background for the classification number if needed to make the number stand out. This area should always be the same distance from the bottom of the book. If the spine is too thin, place the number on the front cover at the lower left-hand corner of the book. (See in chapter 2, Step 7, Purchase Basic Library Supplies, p. 32.)

Place inserts in the book. One of these is the book pocket, on which you should type the call number in the upper left-hand corner; the accession number in the upper right-hand corner; a short title near the top of the pocket. Paste the pocket either slightly below the center of the inside back cover or at the center of the first right-hand page.

Book Pocket

Sample Book Card

201.1
FLY

Man: Ruined and Restored

201.1 FLY	250
Flynn, Leslie B.	
Man: Ruined and Restored	

Another important insert is the book card. On this you should type the call number in the upper left-hand corner; the last name of the author; a short title; accession number in the upper right-hand corner. Then insert the card into the book pocket.

The date due slip is another necessary insert. Paste the slip on the end paper opposite the book pocket. Do not cover up maps, illustrations, or important information on the inside covers. Rather, use one of the blank pages at the end of the book.

If a bookplate is to be inserted, complete the proper information on the plate and paste it on the inside front cover of the book.

Then you are ready to type the catalog cards. (See in chapter 9, Typing the Cards, p. 129.)

Catalog cards must be filed very carefully or they may become lost in the catalog and useless. Details for filing can be found in a cataloging manual.

(See in chapter 9, the Use and Maintenance of the Catalog, p. 132.)

Shelve the Books

Books are arranged on the shelves reading from left to right on each shelf and from top to bottom of each shelf unit. The call numbers must be read carefully in order that like books will be placed together.

7
Selection

For the several steps involved in the flow of work, two areas need to be covered in more detail. The first is the selection of books and the second the cataloging of books. These areas give character and strength to a library. They affect the service performance and the circulation achieved. Both require a certain amount of training to do well.

Personnel for Selection

Materials Selector Coordinator

One person must take the principal responsibility for selection. Because of the importance of the responsibility and the difficulty of the job, it cannot be delegated to just anyone in the congregation. Novices might select books on the basis of personal preference or the looks of a cover or even hearsay.

The choices need to be made by a person who is trained in selection. As information on materials is gathered by the library committee, the selector must guide the thinking of the committee to the most profitable media for the library. Usually the job is undertaken by the librarian.

The selection of materials should not reflect the choices and decisions of just one person. That person may find certain books tedious reading and yet those same books may give great pleasure and profit to many other readers. Or, in the past, that person may have read books that delighted her, but do not have the same appeal anymore. Yet there are many in the congregation who would receive great blessing in reading them.

The leadership of the church should be given an opportunity to make an input with their ideas. This would include the pastoral staff, church board members, Sunday School superintendent and teachers, as well as organizational leaders.

Recommendations should be made by the library committee as they receive information channeled to them. The recommendations should be taken under consideration as to priority of need, a fuller understanding of the book, finances, doctrine and policies of the church.

Qualifications of Selectors

In most churches, we might never find an ideal selector. These qualities are given as guidelines to help those who have the responsibility of selecting books realize the importance of this position and work toward becoming a better selector. Seven qualifications need to be considered for an ideal selector.

Know book titles. She should have a knowledge of the leading titles being currently issued for the religious market. How does a selector gain a familiarity with book titles?

She reads ads, write-ups in magazines, brochures and catalogs; watches for best-seller lists issued by publishers and jobbers; listens to those who are talking about books—people of the church, those who appear on Christian TV and radio programs; spends time in her local Christian bookstore becoming acquainted with the titles on the shelves and those on the new book display.

A good way to store information on books is to write pertinent information about a book on a 3″ x 5″ card or even cut out printed information about it and paste it on a card.

Know religious authors. Again it is more than just knowing the name. Helpful information for the staff and for promotional purposes can be gathered such as:

The kind of books the author writes; his educational background; his ecclesiastical background; his present ministry; his philosophy of Christian living; his style of writing; to what age level or group of people he appeals; his reputation and significance as a Christian writer.

Know religious publishers. When a publisher's name is called to your attention, an ideal selector should be able to tell something about:

The publisher's specialties, strengths and weaknesses; the pluses and minuses of his past publications; what to expect in general from any book coming from the publisher; his theological background and church relationship; the founders' convictions; the publisher's attitude toward contemporary Christian living.

Have you ever considered the responsibility a publisher has? The publisher is a:

• *Middleman.* He coordinates the work of many people. These include the author, editor, designer, typesetter, printer, binder, warehouseman and wholesaler.

• *Book arranger.* He must arrange the book so the ideas in the mind of the author are made public and get to the bookshelves of the home, office and library.

• *Financier.* He must spend quite a bit of money to produce each book. A writer for a manuscript must be found. The manuscript must be edited for spelling, punctuation, bibliography, notes, etc. The copy must be prepared for the printer.

After all this is done, the publisher hopes that enough people will see their need to buy the book, making it worthwhile to publish it from the financial standpoint as well as spiritually.

Know religious subjects. There are many areas in which religious subjects present themselves. When the talk is about religion, Christianity, and the Bible, the selector should have a clear picture of the subjects.

As the selector goes through the classes, divisions and sections of the 200 class of the Dewey Decimal System, she should be able to understand the terms that are used.

A list of social awareness books recently published contained 29 categories. A selector should be acquainted with the terms that deal with this subject.

She should understand theological jargon. Also, she should be aware of which contemporary subjects are on the best-seller lists month by month. Many subjects increase in popularity for a time and then drop off, making way for another subject.

Know the needs of the people of the church. A good selector should be aware of spiritual needs as expressed by individuals in her church. The fact that a book is widely read in one church does not guarantee its acceptance in another.

Those who are involved with selection need to be acquainted with the people of the church in order to be sensitive to their needs. They should be aware of the level of secular and biblical education of the people. In this way, selectors can estimate the reading difficulty of books and match them to the reading skills of the users.

They should choose books that are relevant to needs expressed. To make Bible truths relevant simply means that the reader is established in an understanding of the facts of God's Word and then is shown how to apply those facts to everyday life.

A good selector should promote books by using phrases that show the relevancy of God's Word to the needs of the people. This will help strike a responsive chord in their hearts. She should recognize that there are individual interests as well as common problems and needs.

Someone has said about the intelligent selection of materials in a public library that it involves a lifetime of studying people and materials. The selector in a church library must constantly learn about the people of the church and the materials that are available.

Be impartial in choices. A good selector should maintain freedom from prejudice. She should select materials on the basis of their worth to the reader and not on nonessential matters. Materials are selected that can have meaning for, and an impact on, the lives of many people in the church.

Be trained. Where can a selector get training that will help her be a better worker?

Read books on public library selection located in the public libraries and books on church library selection sold in Christian bookstores. Attend library seminars. Share experiences with other church librarians. Talk to the leadership of the church for their advice on books. Talk to the personnel of the local Christian bookstore. The actual experience of the selector in selecting and evaluating books will help the selector grow in this phase of the library ministry.

Take teacher training courses in the Bible and in understanding people. Make sure you know the policies and doctrines of the church.

To be a good selector is not an easy job. It requires a great deal of time, thought, effort and spiritual knowledge. A number of principles have been given, but the work cannot be done automatically. No special formula exists for successful book selection.

No easy road can be found toward the building of an effective book collection. If the library is to add materials which appeal to the people of the church with their varied backgrounds, their changing interests and needs, selection is going to require much time and knowledge.

(See in chapter 6, Select the Book, p. 87.)

Prepare a Book Selection Policy

Before you open your library, the principles of selection for your library should be compiled in written form called a book selection policy. The policy should be prepared by the library committee. Because of the importance of the selection to the library through the years and to the people of the church, it would be well for the church board to see and approve it.

The policy should include: why and how the library selects the books it does; basis of selection; personnel for selection; criteria for selection; scope of selection—types of materials to be selected; exclusions; gift books; replacements; weeding of books; quantity.

Purpose. State why you are writing the policy, how it affects the library staff and of what benefit it is to those who use the library. The policy will be not only a guide to the choice of books by the library committee, but also a statement about the people it intends to serve or not to serve. Such a policy might prevent a lot of pressure from outside sources to fill the library with materials that would not contribute to its objectives.

Basis. The basis of the selection of materials for your library rests to a great extent on the objectives of your library, what you expect the library to be. The fulfillment of what you expect to do through the library will be dependent on what is selected for the library.

(See in chapter 2, Step 3, Define Library Objectives, p. 26.)

Personnel. State who can make recommendations to the library committee for the selection of materials and who will coordinate the recommendations for selection. (See section in this chapter titled Personnel for Selection, p. 99.)

Criteria for Selection

List the standards that will be used in judging whether or not a book should be entered into the library.

Biblical standards are vital. Is the Bible the basic authority for what is written? Is the book true to the Bible? Does the book present facts accurately? Does it exalt Jesus Christ? Is the doctrine in harmony with the teaching of the church?

Christian living standards too are important. Is the Christian living presented Christlike? Is it relevant to today's living? Is it in harmony with the teaching of the church?

Content standard. This has to do both with quality and quantity of content. Is the quality of mediocre consistency or meaty? What kind of coverage of the subject matter is given? Is it complete or just partial? Does it exhaust the subject or is it selective in the aspect of the subject treated?

• Is it a responsible coverage of the subject matter? Did the author write with authority, sincerity and positiveness? Will the subject interest the potential user?

• Is the quantity of content complete or just partial? Does it exhaust the subject or is it selective? How much information will the reader gain? Does it say it very well? Is it too brief, too wordy?

• Permanency of content is an important consideration. At the end of 12 months, will the content still have value or is it short-lived, not too important a subject?

• Importance of content, too, should be weighed carefully. Will the contents be important to the users or potential users of the library because they need what is given? What is the spiritual value? What is the recreational value? What is its informational value?

• Relevance of content should be considered. Is the material recent enough in light of the subject? Has the work been superceded by one making use of later research? Will the book bring some new, worthwhile information to the library collection?

Writing standards. Not only are you interested in what the book says, but you are also interested in how it says it. Does the book read easily? Do the vocabulary and sentence structure fit the reading abilities of the patrons?

• Does the book have a popular appeal? Some common ideas can be made far more interesting by skillful writers. Does the book communicate effectively? Is it easy to get hold of what the author is writing about? Is the language in the latest style?

• What is the arrangement of the book? Is there a progression from the known to the unknown? Is there a good, logical, chronological, pedagogical, evolutionary, hierarchial arrangement? Are there outlines, summaries, index, table of contents and illustrations?

• Does it present previously collected information in a new arrangement appealing to readers? Are there any unusual features or methods of displaying information? Has the author been creative in presentation? Is the work original or can you read someone else's writing in it?

Production standards should be maintained. Does the book have a quality *cover*? Is the *title* on the cover the kind that will help you "sell" the book to the people? Is the *binding* durable, easy to open, of good workmanship quality? Is the *paper* of good quality? When looking at the print, is the *type face* readable? Is it pleasing to the eye? What about the format of the page? One may say the page is "right" when it is pleasing to look at, when it invites reading.

Cost standards are critically important. Is the price realistic? Does the length warrant the price? How does it compare with other books the same size? Does the quality warrant the price? A book may have a lot of pages and say very little or it may have fewer pages and say much more.

• Does the binding warrant the price? Is it a book that will stand up under much use? Does the subject warrant the price? Are you paying too much for a fading subject, or will the material be of interest for many years?

• Do the overall needs of the library warrant the price of this particular book? Would its purchase prohibit the buying of other books which are more important?

Availability of the subject matter is another consideration. Is it something carried by the public library in detail? Is it a subject that is treated equally well or better in another book? How much depth do you want in your library on any particular subject?

Promotion of the book is important. Are there ads on the book in the Christian magazines your people read? Are reviews of the book appearing in written or audio form? Is the book listed in the catalogs coming across your desk? How does the Christian bookstore rate its acceptance by their clientele?

When your standards have been written, select and buy consistently according to them. Also keep the standards in mind as you weed books from your library.

(See in chapter 11, Criteria for Selection, p. 104.)

The Scope of Selection

Because of the complexity of human nature, differing abilities of people in the church, varied spiritual maturity levels and the various aspects of any subject, variety is important to meet multiple interests.

(See in chapter 12, Developing Readers to Enjoy the Ministry, p. 170.)

Do not select for just the borrowers at the present time. Books should be in the library to serve young children who have to be read to and for every age through the senior citizen, some of whom might also need help in reading.

All-church leadership helps are needed: resource materials, supplementary materials, reference materials for those who are in various positions of leadership.

How many subjects will your library cover? Will you specialize in some of them? What depth of materials will be available on a given subject?

Exclusions from the selection. Certain types of books you may not want to carry in the library. They may be carried in the public library in depth. Their contents indicate they should be excluded. There is a lack of interest in the subject up to this point.

Selection as it affects gift books. Will you accept gift books? If you do, be sure they are judged according to the same standards as purchased books. What will you do with gift books that contain out-dated information, are a duplicate of a book which you already have in sufficient number, are those for which there is little circulation value, or are in poor physical condition? Will you provide a receipt for income tax purposes?

Replacement of books. Perhaps a book has been lost, damaged or worn out. Will it be replaced automatically, evaluated as to its continued value or just forgotten?

Weeding the selection. Weeding is the systematic removal of materials no longer useful or essential to maintaining the purpose and quality of resources. Discard everything that is not relevant to the particular purposes your library is to serve.

This discarding of materials requires the same degree of attention as the initial selection and deserves careful study. What will you do with the books that are worn through use; those that are no longer timely; books that are no longer considered accurate and factual; those that have had little or no use; those that are of questionable value; excess copies of books no longer in demand; or earlier editions of books.

Old books, old editions, duplicates must be justified for they take up space and absorb processing time. Is the book reliable, factual, accurate? Are the materials applicable to today? Does the book have a potential use? Does the book have a historical value? Try to trade or sell discarded books if possible.

Quantity to be selected of any given book. Most librarians are thankful they can buy one copy of a book. Certain exceptions occur when a speaker comes to a church or the majority of people of the church have heard a particular author. Because of the large requests for his book, two or more copies may be needed. Later on the duplicate copies may be sent to missionaries.

Tools for Selection

Certain tools give the selector news of the book world, such as publishing trends, book reviews. Use the tools to help you in your selection.

A number of best-seller lists are available. They will show which books are selling the best on the current market.

Publishers prepare catalogs and brochures for distribution through your local Christian bookstore. Some carry more information on the books than others.

Look for book advertisements and book review columns in general Christian magazines and in your denominational magazine. Also note the subjects being covered by articles in these magazines.

Books and pamphlets giving listings (see bibliography for details of books) include *Books for Christian Educators, The Minister's Library, Books in Print,* and *Current Christian Books.*

The Christian bookstore can become a tool for selection from the standpoint of its displays, information from its employees, and the opportunity to spend time in browsing among books.

Results of good selection. The right material will be provided for the right patron at the right time. Appropriate subject content will be available for the age and interests of all groups served.

The best material will be provided for the largest number at the least cost. The most materials will be secured for the donors' dollars. Materials will be provided for the interests, information and enlightenment of all the people of the church. A live, balanced, up-to-date collection both in subject content and kinds of materials will be provided.

Satisfaction for the reader will be assured. The amount of satisfaction a reader finds in the library depends directly upon the line of books available. If the selector manages to consistently choose books of no interest or use to the readers, the patrons will not be satisfied.

8
Subject Headings and Classification

Talk about "cataloging" a book refers to all the activities involved in preparing a book to take its place in the library. The term is also used to describe any specific part of the work.

Through the years, many detailed cataloging procedures have been established in secular libraries. It would be impossible to fully cover them all. After you have read the basic materials given in chapters 8 and 9, you can obtain more detailed information from books listed in the bibliography.

As indicated in chapter 6, for convenience in understanding, cataloging can best be described in two phases. This chapter will cover *subject cataloging*, in which subject headings and classification numbers are assigned to books. As a result of this effort, books will be grouped on the shelves according to similar characteristics.

Chapter 9 will cover phase 2, called *descriptive cataloging*, in which information is gathered for the library catalog, and the main subject and added entries are determined.

Unless the two phases of cataloging are initiated correctly when the library begins, cataloging someday will become a great task for a librarian trying to "catch up." Patrons will not be able to receive the guidance they should in finding the right materials. Materials may not be placed in their proper position relative to other materials.

Assigning Subject Headings

No matter how many subjects a book may treat, it can be classified and stand on the shelves in only one location. However, it may be entered in the catalog under as many subject headings as are necessary to express the important topics treated in the book.

Many people who come into the library will ask for materials by subject. Therefore it is important to have a good subject catalog. These steps should be followed in assigning subject headings:

Examine the book. With pencil and paper in hand, jot down information that can be used as a basis for determining a subject heading as well as a classification number.

Read the title page, preface, all or part of the introduction. Look over the table of contents. Read part of the book itself. If the library has a book evaluator, her information may be of help to the classifier.

(See in chapter 3, Evaluators, p. 42.)

Any information printed on the back cover of a paperback or the flaps of the book jacket should be read. Ask yourself: What is the book all about; what is the main emphasis of the book; what was the author's purpose in writing the book? Envisage the needs of the readers and to whom the book will be most useful.

List the subject or subjects treated in the book.

Establish a subject heading for the book. There may be several ways to state the primary subject of the book. However, it can be stated by one descriptive term.

The subject heading is that descriptive term composed of a word or phrase. Choosing the correct subject heading terminology for your library is very important. To help you in this:

Do not invent subject headings on the spot. Use a standard subject list. The *Sears List of Subject Headings* is used extensively by public libraries. It is revised about every five years. There is no comparable comprehensive list such as this specifically for the church library manuals.

Become acquainted with terms being currently used by theologians, teachers and authors of Christian books and magazines.

Consider terms that most people using your library would understand and refer to. Ask yourself, Would the patron expect to find the book listed under the heading I have chosen?

Describe the subject by the most specific term possible. Check the catalog to make sure that subject is not being worded in a different way.

Work for uniformity of wording. Use the same subject wording for all headings on the same subject so that they may be brought together in the catalog with uniformity and consistency.

Unless care is exercised as to the word used to describe subject headings, two or more subject headings can have the same meaning. For example, one subject heading could use the word "ecclesiology" and another "church history." Both would be treating the same subject and this would divide the cards so that all books under the same subject would not be shown under one heading.

In order to maintain uniformity and consistency in the subject wording of your catalog, a subject authority file would be very helpful. A card is made for each subject heading used in the catalog. In addition to showing which headings have been used, they also show which references have been made to those headings.

Classification

Classification May Be Thought of in Three Ways:
It is a *system*. Classification is based on a set of principles and rules. It is a logical plan to group similar books.

It is an *arrangement*. An attempt is made to place all knowledge in a logical order to make it easy for people to locate the information they need.

It is an *art*. People who classify must understand how books are arranged in conformity with the system. One learns to classify by classifying.

The Purposes of Classification Are:
To give books a definite place in the library collection. When a classification number is assigned, it becomes the permanent "house number" for the book. Thus every book can be returned to its correct location easily.

To bring similar books together. When put on the shelf according to classification number, books dealing with the same subject will be together. This makes it possible for books to be used in relation to one another.

To bring related books in close proximity. Not only will similar books be together, but books will stand near others with which they can be correlated. In this way, one subject merges into another.

To insert new books with existing books consistently. Shelving should be flexible enough and the classification system broad enough so that new books may be placed in their proper group no matter the size of the library.

To make books more available. Books are classified so they might be used by as many people as possible and meet as many needs as possible.

In order to classify books by subject, some system of classification must be adopted. There are poor systems and there are good systems.

Poor systems and the problems they create include the following:

• No-numbering "system." A tremendous problem arises when a new librarian finds the previous librarian has used no numbering system at all. Now she must catalog all the books as soon as possible.

• Homemade system. This may involve numbers, letters or colors. The problem that arises is that as the library grows, the system is no longer able to handle the number of books involved.

• Dewey Decimal Adaptation. Two problems can arise. The first is that often different adaptations are used by different librarians in the same library, causing confusion. Second, as the library grows in the number of books as well as subject categories, the system is unable to handle the books and subjects involved.

Good systems and the advantages they provide are worth considering. There are several good systems, but the most practical for the average church library is the Dewey Decimal System as provided in the 18th edition of the schedule. Here are some reasons for this view:

Children are learning how to use the Dewey Decimal System in school. More and more publishers are including suggested Dewey Decimal call numbers in their books.

Once the system is understood, it is relatively easy to use. By using the complete schedule, a library can have an indefinite expansion system as well as a continuity of system throughout the years no matter who the librarian is.

The Dewey Decimal System was first published in 1876 and has been revised 17 times. Melvil Dewey was concerned about developing a system in which similar books could be grouped together even if there were thousands or millions of books.

The following titles are used to describe all or part of the classification information:

• *Symbols* that indicate age, biography, reference, size. *Set of numerals* that indicate the classification number. *Letters* that represent the author's identification.

• *Symbols* that indicate the volume number, copy number or date are as follows:

• *Call number.* Uses all of the above information when available. This name relates the number to the book storage area. It had its beginning in the days when books were kept in stacks of shelves which were inaccessible to the public. The patron would request or "call for" the book he had selected by means of the catalog.

• *Notation.* Refers to the set of numerals. This name relates the number to the classification system. Notation refers to the system of numbers and letters used to represent a classification system.

• *Classification number.* Also refers to the set of numerals. This name relates the number to a subject area in the classification system. It tells us that the books are in a special location in the library as reflected by its subject content. It is a complete identification of an individual work and its relative location.

Dewey Decimal principles: Each group in the system always goes from the *general* to the *specific.* Each group is divided on the basis of *10 units.*

• There are 10 *main, broad classes* of knowledge using numbers from 0 through 9. These are represented by the number in the first position of the notation. When writing a class number by itself, we add two zeros to make it a hundred number.

• There are *10 divisions* of each class in tens. These are represented by the number in the second position of the notation. There are a total of 100 divisions.

• There are *10 sections* of each division in units totaling 1,000 sections. These are represented by number in the third position of the notation.

• From here, there are *tens of sub-sections* totaling an innumberable amount. These are represented by the numbers to the right of the decimal point.

• *The ten classes of the system.* This is a brief description of what is found in each of the 10 classes. Entire manuals are written on classification and it would be impossible to include every detail in this general description.

000—*Generalities.* Included in this class are such books as bibliographies, books on the library, general encyclopedias and book rarities.

100—*Philosophy.* Books in this class answer the question, "Who am I?" These books deal with what men think about themselves. It is man's attempt to understand his experiences. Included are books on the mind and body, psychology, etc.

200—*Religion.* Books in this class answer the question, "Who made me?" They deal with what man thinks about God. This is man's belief in the supernatural.

300—*Sociology.* Books in this class answer the question, "Who is my neighbor?" These books deal with what man thinks about other people. It is man's relationship with others. It is how men live together. Included are books on political science, law and education.

400—*Philology.* This word simply means the study of language. It answers the question, "How can I make men understand me?" Here are books telling how men communicate through sound and written symbols. This class includes books on languages, dictionaries and grammars. In the church library, books dealing with Greek and Hebrew would be placed in this section.

500—*Natural or pure science.* Books in this class answer the question, "What do we see in nature?" Here are books on understanding nature and the world about us. It is man's study of the laws of nature. Such areas as mathematics, astronomy, biology and zoology are included.

600—*Applied or useful science or useful arts.* Books in this class answer the question, "How can we use what we know about nature?" It is man's way of making use of the knowledge of nature for his own comfort and convenience. Books included are on medicine, agriculture, mechanics, trades and building.

700—*Fine arts.* Answers the question, "How can I enjoy my leisure time?'' Such subjects as gardening, art, photography and music tell how.

800—*Literature*. These books answer the question, ''What has man done in the past?'' The writing has excellence of form and expression. The ideas express permanent and/or universal interest.

900—*History*. Books in this class answer the question, ''How can I leave a record for men of the future?'' These books record all the past history of mankind, the discoveries about the surface of the earth and its history before he came to live in it. Books included are on geography, travel, biography and history of the various areas of the world.

The ten divisions of the religion class. Because most of the church library books are located in the 200 class, this class shall be noted more in detail as our example of the Dewey Decimal System.

200—*General works*. Here are such books as dictionaries, encyclopedias and concordances of religion.

210—*Natural theology or religion*. These books relate to a philosophical concept of the topics covered rather than a Christian viewpoint. Here are such things as concepts of God, science and religion, and the nature and place of man on the universe.

220—*Bible*. Here are commentaries on the Bible as a whole, the Old Testament, the New Testament, as well as the Apocrypha.

230—*Christian doctrinal theology*. Specific doctrines concerning God, Jesus Christ, salvation, and future things.

240—*Christian moral and devotional theology*. Theology that is expressed in devotional literature, evangelistic literature, personal and family religion.

250—*Local Christian church*. Homiletics, church government and administration, parochial schools.

260—*Christian social and ecclesiastical theology*. Public worship, missions, Christian education.

270—*Organized Christian church*. Various historical periods of the church, special topics of church history, the church in the various continents of the world.

280—*Denominations and sects*. A study from the historical and geographical aspect.

290—*Other religions*. Comparative religions, classical religions and various religions.

The ten sections of the Bible division.

220—*Bible as a whole.* The origin of the Bible, concordances, dictionaries and commentaries on the whole Bible.

221—*Old Testament in general.* Geography, chronology of the Old Testament as well as biographies of Old Testament characters.

222—*Historical books of the Old Testament.* Genesis through Esther.

223—*Poetical books of the Old Testament.* Job through the Song of Solomon.

224—*Prophetical books of the Old Testament.* Isaiah through Malachi.

225—*The New Testament in General.* The geography, history, chronology of the New Testament as a whole and biographies of New Testament characters.

226—*The Gospels and Acts.* Matthew through the Book of Acts.

227—*The Epistles.* Romans through Jude.

228—*The Revelation.*

229—*The Apocrypha.*

The sub-sections of the 227 section—the epistles.

.1—Romans

.2—1 Corinthians

.3—2 Corinthians

.4—Galatians

.5—Ephesians

.6—Philippians

.7—Colossians

.8—Pastoral epistles. 1 Thessalonians through Hebrews.

.9—Catholic or general epistles. James through Jude.

Sub-sections of the 227.8 section—other Pauline epistles.

.81—1 Thessalonians

.82—2 Thessalonians

.83—1 Timothy

.84—2 Timothy

.85—Titus

.86—Philemon

.87—Hebrews

Special categories include fiction books, arranged according to the first three letters of the author's last name. Precede with the letter *F* for adult fiction or *Fj* for junior fiction.

Bible biographies are numbered thusly: collective—220.92; individual, Old Testament—221.924; individual, New Testament (except Jesus Christ and His family)—225.924.

Missionary biographies are numbered 226.092.

Other biographies are numbered as follows: individual—B; collective—920.

Biography books do not use authors' identification, but rather the first three letters of the last name about whom the book was written.

Reference books are consulted for a definite fact or piece of information. They are kept in a special reference section for use in the library only. All books have a letter R preceding their call number.

Books too large to be placed with other books in their section can be shelved in a separate section. In this case precede the call number with a letter *q*.

Children's books use these letters as part of their classifciation: *e*—easy or picture books (for children up to 5); *c*—children's books (for ages 5 through 9); *j*—junior books (for ages 9 through 12); *t*—teen books (over 12 years of age.). *Fc*—children's fiction books.

There are two types of classification:

Broad classification. This is the grouping of books in classes or divisions without recognizing the more minute subdivisions. In other words, instead of using numbers to the right of the decimal point, the number is reduced to the three numbers to the left of the decimal point. Small libraries may find it advantageous to reduce the classification number to the most specific three-digit number.

Close classification. This is the arrangement of subjects in detailed subdivisions under a class or division. In this case up to three or four numbers could be used to the right of the decimal point.

Steps in determining the classification number. The person who has assigned the subject headings has examined the book, listed the subjects and established a subject heading for the book. Now she is ready to take two more steps in connection with classification.

Use the tools that are available. Every classifier needs to avail herself of the Dewey Decimal classification schedule. It comes in three volumes:

Vol. 1—An introduction to the system with important tables; Vol. 2— The schedules; Vol. 3—The relative index—an alphabetical list of all the main headings found in the DDC schedule.

If the library can afford the three volumes, that is fine. However the 200 class has been printed by Broadman in a separate volume. This can be used for the majority of books, and for those that have to do with other classes the librarian can consult the complete schedule at her local public library. The classifier should become thoroughly acquainted with the system.

When classifying, the classifier can go direct to the schedule to deter-

Practice Sheet For Classifying Books

Title _____
Subject(s) _____

	Title	Number
Class		
Division		
Section		
Subdivision(s)		

Author _____
                  (last name)   (first 3 letters)
Special grouping _____
Call number _____
                 (number) (initials) (special)

First position
Second position
Third position

	Title	Number
Class	Religion	200
Division	Bible	220
Section	Epistles	227
Sub-section	Romans	227.1
Author	Wiersbe	WIE

Call number:	Close classification would use	227.1	WIE
	Broad classification would use	227	WIE

mine the proper number, or she may go through the relative index as found in Volume 3. However, one should never class solely from the index.

The seasoned classifier will go through these steps automatically, but the beginner will find that practicing with the form will help her to think through the number clearly.

Assign a valid classification number. This will represent the place you think the book will be most useful. When a book appears to belong equally in two places in the classification, the classifier must use her good judgment in making a proper decision.

When a book deals with two or three divisions of a subject, place it in the one which appears to be the most important. If they are of equal importance, then use the first one treated.

When a subject arises for which there is no place provided in the classification scheme, find the heading to which it seems to be most nearly related. Make a place for it there.

9
The
Catalog

The previous chapter noted the first phase of cataloging a book in which a subject heading was determined for the book and a classification number assigned to the book. This chapter deals with gathering information and preparing the cards to build the catalog.

The catalog is a very important part of the library development and ministry, and should be built very carefully. In almost all church libraries, the catalog is in a card form using a cabinet of trays or drawers.

Defining the Card Catalog

The card catalog can be defined as an inventory, information and location record.

It is a total list of books and other materials in the library. Each entry for any given item is typed on a separate 3″ × 5″ card. The list answers such questions as these:

Does the library carry a book or some other medium with a certain *title?* Do you have the book, *What Happens When Women Pray?*

Does the library carry materials by a certain *author or artist?* Or, what is the most recent book by....? What books do you have written by Warren Wiersbe? Has he prepared any other material in any other media?

What books or other media does the library carry on a certain *subject?*

What materials in any media do you have on the subject of creation?

What is the *age* or *edition* of an item? How recent is the book *Cults, World Religions and You?*

What is the book all *about?* With what does the book *God Can Make It Happen* have to do?

Information record. After discovering the library has a book with a title, author or subject in which you are interested, you might want to know a little about the book to see if it has possibilities for your needs. The information placed on the main entry card will draw attention to the purpose of the item, its contents and its relation to other works.

Location record. Once you have determined the book looks like it is what you need, the next question is, Where is the item located? The catalog is an index to the materials to help you find any item quickly.

As the cataloger gathers information, she will use that data to determine the following information for the catalog card:

The subject(s) covered in the book. As stated in chapter 8, the cataloger is to be a subject specialist. She reveals the subjects covered in each book.

A description of the book. The cataloger is a discoverer of helpful information about the book. She not only discovers that the book is on a certain major subject, but finds hidden bits of information which may be buried between its covers.

A cataloger must remember she is trying to describe the contents and the make-up of each book for those who come into the library. She makes available the major points with regard to the contents of the book to help users of the catalog discover what they need.

The more the material in the book can be characterized, the more valuable the content will be to more people. This description is put on the catalog card according to the accepted catalog rules.

She decides under whose name the book will appear. She also identifies the book by its features or unique characteristics. She must be able to describe a book in such a way that a reader can visualize the volume—its size, date of publication, publisher, etc. She may indicate the type of reader for whom the book has been written.

An interpretation of the book. The cataloger is an interpreter of the book. She is constantly studying, recording and interpreting books. She not only reads what a book says to her, but what it will say to others. She interprets what the author is trying to say, to present the point of view of the author.

Relationships with other books. The cataloger is a placer of books. She brings together a record of those books which treat the same subject and arranges the whole card catalog so that the books may be used comparatively.

Tools for Cataloging

Cataloging manual. As suggested earlier, a person doing cataloging should have a book to help with subject headings, and a book to help with classification.

A third book is needed for general cataloging which will specialize in building the catalog. *Commonsense Cataloging: A Manual for the Organization of Books and Other Materials in Schools and Small Public Libraries* is such a book (see appendix for details).

In the preface, the author states: "Church libraries were not included in the original planning of this manual, but it developed that, with few exceptions, the practices recommended would also be suitable for church and parish libraries; these exceptions are therefore noted in the text." The book includes cataloging information not only for book media, but also for audiovisual media.

Publishers' information. More and more publishers are putting information for the cataloger on the back of the title page. Some reproduce the information found on the Library of Congress card. Scripture Press lists a suggested Dewey Decimal classification number plus subject headings for each book.

Unit card system. A set of identical printed cards made according to standard library cataloging rules to be used in the card catalog can be purchased from the Library of Congress or other sources. Each card contains the complete main entry information.

One card will be used for the main entry card and another for the shelf card. The balance of the cards will be used for added and subject entries. You will see many of these in your public library, but because of the expense involved not many church libraries can afford to buy the sets.

Information for the Catalog Cards

The Main Entry Card

This is usually the card giving the name of the author on the entry line. If there is no author, the corporate body responsible for the book can be used. It is the principal card from which all other entries for the book are made.

The main entry card is valuable from two aspects: It enables a patron to find out what an author has written. It makes it possible for the staff to see by the tracings what other catalog cards have been made on the book.

The categories of information needed on the card are the *call number*, made up of classification number, first three letters of the author's last name, and any special information symbols; also the *main entry word or phrase*.

If there is an *author*, type his name the same way it appears on the title page. Birth and death dates may be used if desired. If there are *two or three authors* use the first name on the title page.

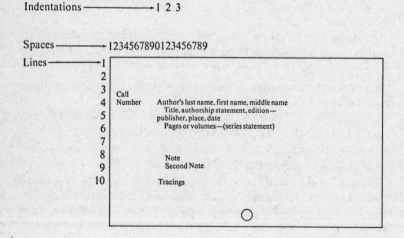

Book Main Entry Skeleton Card

Indentations ———————→ 1 2 3

Spaces ————→ 1234567890123456789

Lines ————→ 1
2
3   Call
4   Number   Author's last name, first name, middle name
5   Title, authorship statement, edition—
6   publisher, place, date
              Pages or volumes—(series statement)
7
8   Note
9   Second Note
10   Tracings

If there is no author, and if available, use the editor, the compiler, or the name of the corporate body responsible for the book. If all of the above are missing, use the *title*.

The title statement includes the full title of the book as it appears on the title page; information describing *joint responsibility* of authorship such as joint authors and editors, translators, etc. Sometimes this is called the authorship statement.

Also, the edition, sometimes called the edition statement. For example, a book may be in its second revised edition. This implies there are some changes in the text since it was first published. It may be a new edition of a book already in the library.

The imprint includes place of publication—city, state (not necessary in the case of prominent cities); publisher's name (can be shortened to its popular name); date of publication or copyright date.

The collation includes the number of pages *or* the number of volumes (both are not given); illustration information (optional); size of the book (optional).

Series note. A series is a number of separate works, usually related to

Example of Workslip (written in longhand)

```
201.1   Flynn, Leslie B.
Fly
            Man: Ruined and Restored   Victor ©1978
            132 p -- (The Victor Know and Believe
            Series 8 vols, edited by Bruce Shelley)

            Answers the main questions: Where do I
            come from? Why am I here? Where am I
            going?
                  Leader's guide available
            1. Anthropology  2 Sin 3. Genesis
            I Title II Shelley
```

one another in subject or otherwise, issued in succession, normally by the same publisher and in uniform style with a collection title.

Notes are placed on the card to: describe the book or make an explanation of what is in the book; list and/or explain the history or content of the book; show the book's relation to other works; indicate a bibliography in the book with the paging.

Tracings comprise a record of any added or subject entry cards that have been made. The tracings tell how many and what cards exist for each work in order to find them again. If corrections need to be made, or withdrawals from the collection, the cataloger knows where to find all the cards that pertain to the book.

As the cataloger gathers the above information, she writes it on a slip. All cards then can be typed by, saving valuable time for the cataloger.

Added Entry Cards Include the Following:

Title card. This card makes it possible for the patrons to have information under every title in the library. To be included on the card are: title; call number; author's name.

Joint author card. If a book is written by two or three people, the first name is selected for the main entry card. Then an added entry card is made for at least one additional author.

Joint editor card. If a book is written by two or three editors, the first is selected for the main entry card. An added entry card is made for at least one additional editor listing his name along with "jt. ed.".

Series card. A series entry is made when an individual publication has been cataloged as a complete and separate work, but also belongs to a series of importance.

Subject cards. Under subject cataloging, it was discovered that not only is a valid classification number assigned to a book, but also the subjects of the book are listed. No matter how many subjects a book may treat, it can be classified and stand on the shelves in only one place. However, it may be entered in the catalog under as many subject headings as are necessary.

Because of the complex nature of some books, several subject headings may be covered in one book. Many people who come into the library

Added Entry Book Skeleton Cards

Title Card

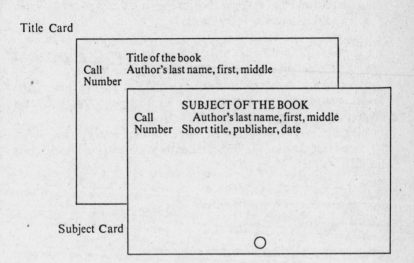

Subject Card

Fiction
and
children's
picture
book
skeleton
Cards

will ask for material by subject. Therefore it is important to have a good subject file.

Cross Reference Cards Include Three Different Types:

Special reference cards. When there is more than one way to word the subject of a book, the cataloger chooses one term that is most familiar to people and then refers to other terms.

This card *refers* the reader from a subject term with which he is acquainted, and which he uses to look for materials related to that subject but which is not used in the catalog, to a term which is used.

This card *directs* the reader from one term to an equivalent term. The reader must *follow* this direction if he is to see what is available on the subject for which he is looking.

"See also" reference cards. This card *refers* the reader from a subject term used in the catalog to one or more terms that are also used to describe the same subject.

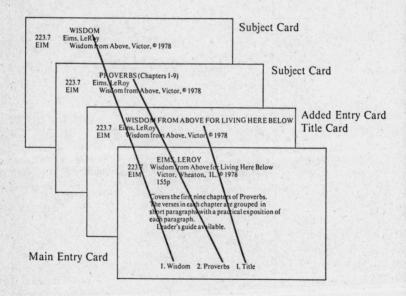

Cross Reference Skeleton Cards

"see"
card

Term not used (in the catalog)

  see

Term used (in the catalog)

○

"see also"
card

Term used

  see also

   OTHER TERMS

○

Book Main Entry Skeleton Card

These terms will *lead* the reader from a term with a wider meaning to a term with a more specific meaning; or from a term with a limited meaning to a term with a wider meaning.

The reader does not have to follow the references. They are offered only as helpful suggestions. Do not make one of these cards unless the term referred to is used in the catalog.

General reference cards. These cards are to guide readers from a term to: a certain special file of materials; a whole class of other terms.

Typing the Cards
The following suggestions for typing cards are based on rules set up by

libraries through the years. It is a good practice for a library to use an established set of rules and make all cards conform to them. When typing cards, reference is made to:

Lines—typewriter lines are always figured from the top edge of the card.

Indentations—typewriter spaces figured from the left edge of the card: 2 spaces in—used to begin the call number; 10 spaces in—1st indentation (also called the author indentation); 12 spaces in—2nd indentation (also called the title and paragraph indentation); 14 spaces in—3rd indentation (also called the description indentation).

Paragraph—a section of the card that deals with a particular point such as the title paragraph, collation, and notes. Each paragraph begins on a new line at the second indentation.

The main entry card and shelf list card. Call number elements include the classification number (3rd line, 2nd space); author's initials (4th line, 2nd space); additional information (5th line, 2nd space).

Main entry word or phrase: 3rd line, 1st indentation; author's last name first, a comma, one space, first name, middle name, dates of the author (optional). If the entry line is too long and must continue on a second line, begin it at the 2nd indentation.

The title statement. The full title of the book is begun one line below the entry line; 2nd indentation. Omit if the title is being used as the main entry phrase only. The first word and proper names are capitalized.

Follow the title with a space, comma, space and type the authorship statement. Follow the statement with a period, space, comma, space and type the edition statement.

When continuing the title statement to the next line, begin it at the 1st indentation.

The imprint. Begin two spaces after the end of the title statement in the same paragraph. Type: place: Publisher, date. If the date is the copyright date, precede it with a letter *c*.

If the imprint must be continued on another line, begin it at the first indentation.

The collation. Begin one line below the end of the imprint information; 2nd indentation. Type: pages (or volumes): illustration and size information is optional.

If the collation must be continued to the next line, begin it at the first indentation.

Series note. Follow the collation information with two spaces and give the series statement in parenthesis. If necessary to continue on the next line, begin at the 1st indentation.

Notes. Begin the first note two lines below the end of the series statement; 2nd indentation. Each note begins a new paragraph at the 2nd indentation.

Lines for each note which are too long and must continue on a second line, begin at the 1st indentation.

Tracings. Begin at least three lines below the notes; 1st indentation. Use a roman numeral for each added entry designation. Use an arabic number for each subject entry designation.

If necessary, tracings can be continued on the back side of the card, near the bottom, by using the word "over" on the front side of the card.

(See chapter 6 for added information on the shelf list card.)

Added entry and subject entry cards may contain less information than what appears on the main entry card.

Title card includes: call number: 3rd line, two spaces in; author's name in full: 3rd line, 1st indentation; title is typed on the line above the author's name, 2nd indentation.

On the *joint authorship card,* joint author is typed one line above the author; 2nd indentation.

Subject card includes call number: 3rd line, 2nd space in; author's name: 3rd line, 1st indentation; a short title: 4th line, 2nd indentation; publisher: same paragraph, dot and space; date: same paragraph; comma and space.

The subject is typed on the line above the author's name in capital letters; 2nd indentation.

Cross reference cards should be prepared as follows:
- *"See" reference card:* Term not used: 3rd line; 2nd indentation. Capitalize all words. Word "see": 5th line; 3rd indentation. Not capitalized. Term used: 7th line; 1st indentation.
- *"See also" reference card:* Term used: 3rd line; 2nd indentation. Words "see also": 5th line; 3rd indentation. Not capitalized. Other terms

used to describe the same subject: 7th and following lines; 1st indentation. Capitalize all words.

Fiction and children's book cards should include: call number. If the book is designated for a certain age or grade level (e.g., *J* for junior readers, or as a reference book, *R*) the symbol can be put on the 2nd line, two spaces in. Author, full name: 3rd line; 1st indentation. Short title: 4th line; 2nd indentation. Date: two spaces after end of title.

No subject cards are made for fiction and children's books.

Use and Maintenance of the Catalog

Drawers should never be more than ¾ full. This allows enough space for cards to be pushed back and forth and remain fully exposed.

Cleanliness. Clean cards should be in the drawers. If some get soiled, replace them.

Keep cards up to date. If a book is removed, make sure all cards related to the book are removed.

Place vital information on each card. Keep in mind the importance of what goes into the catalog. The better the information on the card, the more valuable the card catalog.

Place cards in file accurately. Misfiled cards may make some book useless to those who are looking for its help.

Determine the best arrangement of cards for your library. In the dictionary card catalog, an alphabet is used for all materials. All cards are filed by the first or filing name or word on the card. All cards are interfiled in this order:

• *Book cards*—i.e., the author, title, subject cards for books. Audiovisual cards—i.e., the author, performer or speaker, artist; title card and the subject card for each audiovisual. Cross reference cards.

In the divided card catalog, the author, title and subject cards are put into different tray units. In one arrangement, the author, title and subject cards would each be put in a different tray unit. Another arrangement would be to put the author and title cards in one tray unit while the subject cards would be put in another tray unit.

• *Guide cards.* These cards are made to mark off the catalog with a letter, name or term indicating the kind of catalog cards that follow. To begin with, the guides may be very close together if the catalog is small. However, as the catalog grows, cards should be placed about every one or one and one-half inches apart.

The cards can be purchased with blank tabs on which the wording can be typed. The half-cut cards have the tabs in two positions. The third-cut cards have the tabs in three positions. The fifth-cut cards have the tabs in five positions.

Instruct patrons. Those who use the library should realize the importance of the catalog and be given instruction on how to use it and preserve it.

10
Promotion

Promoting the church library is a key activity for the circulation of materials. A church may have a beautiful library with hundreds of books and audiovisuals, but without promotion much of the money spent on these materials will be wasted because of inactivity.

Promotion must begin even before the library opens. If promotion is discontinued or is not done on a consistent basis, the activity of the library will be affected.

Purposes of Promotion

To motivate people to use the library. Because of the small percentage of people who use the church library, most attenders in the average church have no idea what the library is all about. They have no appreciation of the resources that are available for their use by just coming into the library. People must be given a reason to come to the library where they can be exposed to the materials.

To capture the attention of people. Today radio, television and recordings have the attention of a large percentage of the people who attend our churches. Activities of all kinds such as traveling, participation in special events, or being spectators or participants in sports capture the time of many.

Numerous things on Sunday morning can capture church attenders' attention—activities going on at church, personal problems and needs that weigh heavily on their minds, their children and meeting other people.

As a vital organization of the church, the library should be called to the attention of all the people as an important church function and as an active, contributing part of church life rather than the stagnant organization which people often have considered it to be. Various facets of the library should be brought to the attention of people on a regular basis. People can't use what they don't know about.

To build a reputation for service. Promotion will help you "sell" your library as a place where people can receive help. They can be told of the services you perform and the assistance you offer.

An effective library is one that changes. It is alive. It grows bigger and better and has more special services to offer.

The people of the church change. They find new needs in themselves. They seek new answers, new activities, new people, new places. Because of this, people must constantly have the library ministry presented to them to help meet their current needs.

One of the difficulties with a self-service library is that it can become very cold because the warmth of a personality is not present. The resources that can be discovered by a helping hand are not discovered. It cannot add that vital ingredient to the atmosphere of the library—loving service.

Full service libraries are geared to doing for others. Their motto is: "We're here to help you. We're willing to sacrifice our time because we feel this is an important ministry. We are willing to share our lives with yours." The service your library gives is the life-blood of the library.

To increase traffic to the library. In selling, sometimes the phrase is used, "The more you tell, the more you sell." Promotion will insure a more continuous flow of people and a more loyal group of people coming in.

To make people knowledgeable about Christian literature. As people see and hear what the library has through promotion, they will be learning about the many resources that are available to them. Christian literature of all kinds will be promoted and individuals will be stimulated to use them.

The values of reading will be demonstrated, such as helping people know and understand what is happening in Christendom today; gain personal spiritual satisfaction; meet the practical demands of Christian living; become better Christian workers; and improve their inter-personal relations.

To foster a personal relationship between the library and the people of the church. Some of the things that need to be explained are:

The organization and function of the library; where the finances come from and how they are used; recent problems and successes the library has had; how the library was founded.

Also, how the library has figured in church affairs; what the personnel of the library actually do; how the various departments of the library function; what services the library provides and why.

Also, the library policies regarding book selections; the what and why of library operations; policies such as fines, overdue notices, closed status, check out of books, hours of operation; plans, hopes and dreams about a better tomorrow for the library.

To answer these questions:

• The *why* of the library—why is it in existence? Tell the purpose of the library.

• The *what* of the library—what can it do for individuals? Tell how the materials can benefit people.

• The *how* of the library—how can it be used? Tell the policies of the library.

As your church becomes more and more aware of what you are doing for them, and plan to do for them in the future, the leadership as well as the general membership will be more likely to be sympathetic to library needs.

To push books. One of the main ministries of the library is to sell people on the importance of Christian books. They may be newly arrived books; best-selling books; unusual groups of books; books on current events or books based on special events; as well as books that will contribute to spiritual growth.

As you let people know what the library is all about, they may not hear you the first or second time. So keep telling. The ministry of the library must be impressed upon the minds of all the people of the church so that when a need arises, they will think "library." The people of the church need to be kept up to date on what is new in printed and audiovisual media.

The Person for Promotion

Because of the magnitude and possibilities of library promotion, someone should be given the responsibility of promotion who has no other church duties. Some of the characteristics that will mark an ideal promotional chairman are:

Professionalism. She must learn to effectively think public relations. In fact, all staff members have no other reason to serve except to fulfill entirely the library needs of others. They are to constantly think of what the library can give rather than what it can preserve.

Enthusiasm. She must be enthusiastic in her work. One cannot give the potential library users the spark that will ignite them if she does not have the spark herself.

Knowledge. She must be knowledgeable about what is in the library. She cannot inform if she does not know what the library has to offer. She must be aware of all materials in order to bring them to the attention of the people. In fact she must know every aspect of the library ministry well.

Observant. She must keep her eyes open for new ways to bring the library to the attention of people of all ages.

Concerned. She must love the library ministry. Without loving books, all the public relations in the world will not persuade many people that the library has what they want.

Think big. This is not to suggest carnal boasting, but rather believing and proclaiming that this is a vital ministry in the sight of God and can be used to assist in the growth of the church and its people.

Use people to promote. People are interested in people. You see this demonstrated in TV commercials. In Christian bookstores, perhaps as high as 80 percent of the sales of books is made through the recommendation of others. Depend on people, satisfied persons, to help you promote.

Plug the new. Promote new services, new books, new users, new methods and new activities.

Be interested in individuals. Library promotion should be person-to-person communication.

Planning for Promotion

A very helpful tool to make promotion more effective is a yearly promotional calendar.

Its purpose is to give definite direction to the yearly promotion; to make the library program coincide with the church program. This requires knowing what the church will be doing in the coming year.

Also, it will promote library objectives. It will reflect what the library wants to accomplish, and give a basis for a promotional budget. After the calendar has been completed, costs can be estimated. This will become part of the overall library budget.

The calendar will give a basis for the selection of materials. The materials must be on hand to do the promotion. If they are not in the library already, or are not there in sufficient quantities, materials will have to be ordered. The calendar will help to have variety in the selection and promotion of books. It can help divide the work load, responsibilities can be assigned.

Its development. Purchase a loose-leaf notebook using $8\frac{1}{2}'' \times 11''$ paper. Make a tentative calendar for the entire year including the following items for each month's promotion:

Emphasize the topic you want to stress or highlight during the month. Get ideas from church events, special days, holidays and the seasons of the year. Ask the entire church staff to give you ideas—the pastor, the DCE, the Sunday School superintendent, youth sponsors, etc. As many areas and age levels of the church as possible should be involved in giving ideas for the emphasis.

The aim for each month indicates why you want to make a particular emphasis. It tells what you expect to accomplish through stressing a particular topic. Here are a few suggestions as far as emphases and aims are concerned. Fit them into your church program. They are ideas only.

January: Summer Bible teaching ministries; to provide assistance to the workers in the summer outreach program through various media. (See in chapter 12, Christian Education Emphasis, p. 178.)

February: Christian patriotism; to provide media that reflect and encourage Christian patriotism, or media that warn against forces that would destroy our country. (See in chapter 12, The church narthex, p. 176.)

March: The person and work of Jesus Christ; to provide media on the life and teachings of Christ that will help individuals have a better knowledge of Him. (See in chapter 12, The church auditorium, p. 176.)

April: Church library month; to promote the library to the entire church. Let everyone know about the services and materials of their church library.

National Library Week falls in April. In January, check with your public library for the exact current date. Public libraries will have special events planned throughout the week.

This is a good time for the church library to be promoted. Stress the use of the library as a place for learning and receiving materials for enjoyment as well as profit. Promote such projects as encouraging children to find books and other reference materials in the library on special subjects that particularly interest them.

May: Help for parents of the church; to reach homes with media from the library to be used in counseling, family devotions, parental instruction, etc.

June: An increased reading of books by everyone; to accelerate the reading of Christian books through the summer by means of reading contests.

July: Reaching children of the community; to present Christ to children through books in order to win them to the Saviour.

August: Families reading Christian books; to get families to take paperback books with them on their vacation.

September: A missionary reading program; to deepen the interest of individuals in missions.

October: Reading Christian books; to motivate people who are not reading to get started by asking everyone to read at least one book this month.

November: The giving of books at Christmas; to get people to give a gift with a spiritual emphasis along with their material gift by placing a paperback book with each present.

December: Time for new books in a new year; to motivate people to review their reading habits and encourage them to renew their efforts to take time to read in the new year.

(See chapter 12 for more ideas about emphases and aims.)

Method. The way in which the topic is to be emphasized will greatly affect the way the message is received.

Personnel assignment. Assign the responsibility to do each month's promotion. Try to enlist new people in this aspect of the library ministry. Young people can make posters, displays and use their creativity. Shut-ins can help with copy.

Material needed. In order to build a display, prepare a poster, print a brochure, etc., materials will be needed to do the job right. This must be thought through and listed with each promotion.

Its performance. After the tentative ideas have been completed for the year, begin work on the details of at least the next three months. The promotional chairman should supervise the preparation of each promotion and follow through on the jobs that need to be done.

Media for Promotion

Three general types of media may be used: displays; printed media; other audiovisuals.

Displays

Of all the media, displays have the advantage of using the actual materials to support the topic that is to be publicized. In a display, the book or other item "speaks for itself." People can see and touch it.

Publishers spend thousands of dollars developing book covers, attractively packaging materials and providing informative covers for visual aids. The color, illustrations, and design on book covers have been assembled for one main purpose—to delight the eye of the beholder.

Jacket blurbs are written deliberately to stimulate the potential reader's desire to buy. Displays let the librarian take advantage of these points of sale to help "sell" people on borrowing a book or audiovisual.

Purpose of displays. An effective display must have a clear purpose. Displays are not constructed just to have displays. A message must be conveyed. A message without spoken words, a message visualized, can have more of an impact than even a spoken message.

Such a message catches the attention of people. You have studied the reading needs of the people of your church. You have prayed and asked God what subjects should be brought to the attention of the people of your church. Now you want to get their attention in order for them to get the message.

Display messages help people think about the library. The minds of people ordinarily are occupied with thoughts of where they are going, who they must see, things they must do. Who takes thought of the library or any library materials before they leave home, while they are at church, or as they leave to return home?

Many things catch the attention of people—other people want their attention; the church bulletin gets their attention; the music gets their attention. You want the people of the church to take time to consider the materials you have in your library and what they can do for them.

The display helps people "hear" the message of the library. A display in a store window is to catch your eye and call your attention to the fact that the store carries certain items. You too build a display to call to the attention of people that the library has certain items that will be of help to them.

People are attracted by the things they see. You want to attract to the library people who would not otherwise take notice. Often people do not "see"—they pass right by. You want to stop them.

A good teacher uses a visual aid to catch the attention of the listener whose mind might have been straying. A display is a 3-D visual to catch the attention of the person passing by so that he might "hear" what the library has to say.

Good displays help attract new users to the library. As a person looks at the display, he becomes convinced that a certain book should be read and so he borrows it. Previous users also are attracted to the library. They are reminded as well as motivated to borrow another book.

A list of the various subjects covered by the material in the library could be distributed to the people of the church. But this would not be nearly as effective as a series of displays on the same subjects.

When preparing a display, answer these questions: Why should the book get anyone's attention? In two or three sentences tell what message each book conveys. What action do you want the observer to take about the book? What do these books tell about your library?

Communicates a vital message. When you have the attention of people, then you want to say something of value to them. Picture yourself putting a display in the narthex of your church. Why are you doing it? You want the display to say something important to everyone who passes by, and speak it well.

It will communicate quietly so that it is no noise factor in the area. It will communicate constantly so that no matter when anyone passes by, if they look, they will see its message. It will communicate objectively so that the passerby can think about what he sees and can determine what he should do about it without coercion.

Communicates a specific message. It will give information about specific titles. Materials are made more personal and meaningful. When you look at a shelf of books, sometimes you actually see nothing specific unless you take the books off the shelf one by one. But take six or eight of those books off the shelf and use them in a display, then they will be seen.

Coordinated titles also can be featured. The department store display shows a man's suit with a coordinated shirt and tie. The display accentuates one suit that perhaps would not have been seen when hanging with hundreds of others. The coordinates give added incentive to buy the suit. When several books on one topic are displayed, they complement one another and give greater stimulus for borrowing.

Exclusive titles may be displayed. Some books contain thrilling material, in-depth material, and necessary material that cannot be found elsewhere. But the book stays on the shelf because people are not aware of it and what it contains. Had the book been placed in a display, people would have been made aware of its tremendous contents.

Older titles also can be featured. Perhaps you have been blessed by a book published 25 years ago, but are disappointed that no one seems to borrow it. Put it in a display and see what happens. Older books that do not have the glittering titles, shining jackets, or the contemporary authors may have great content.

Put them in a display with color and descriptive props. You probably will find people borrowing the books and then coming to you and saying, "I'm glad you let me know about that great book!"

Presents a necessary message. The message you want to communicate is that the library has materials to meet the needs of the one looking at the display. The display is saying, "Teacher, do you want to be a better teacher? Here is something that will help."

Or, "Mother and Dad, do you want to do a better job as a parent? Here is something that will help you." Displays show people that help for the satisfying of their needs can be found in the library.

Some books reflect needs. You can find out what the needs are by reviewing subjects in the Dewey Decimal System. For example, there is a need for a deeper prayer life, salvation, dedication of life, knowing about a certain doctrine, etc. When you know the needs, plan displays to meet those needs.

Have you noticed that a manufacturer does not sell a bed as such, but rather asserts that he can meet the need for a good night's rest? Paint is not sold, but the manufacturer has the answer to how one can have the beautiful-looking house he wants. In a year's time, in any given display area, materials could be shown that will help meet 25-30 major needs of people.

Reinforces a message. Insert a message in the church bulletin about books. Reinforce it with a display. Put up a poster on a certain subject, support it with a display. The bulletin board carries the message; the display has the actual materials.

The pastor preaches a message on prayer. A display can reinforce his message through a presentation of books on prayer.

The Sunday School teacher is teaching on the Book of Daniel. A display makes appropriate resource material available to the class members.

Books taken from displays can make the message from both the pulpit and the Sunday School class more meaningful and may contribute to greater participation.

Motivates people to action. A display should get people to do something about what they have heard and seen. You want to get people excited enough about the materials displayed for them to take and make use of some of the items.

Displays go to people. Sometimes it is difficult to get people to walk to the library and get materials that will help them on a particular subject. It is much easier when we take the materials to the people.

Displays instruct people. Sometimes it is difficult to get people to look in the subject catalog or go through the books on the shelf in a certain section. It is much easier to help people if we put those same books in a nice display area, separate them from the rest of the collection and dress up the display area.

Displays remind people. Sometimes people are too busy even to think of what they could get to help them. A display comes to them and reminds them of the helps available, thus encouraging quicker decisions.

Develops the image of the library. It is important to have neat displays or people will say, "That library operation sure must be a mess."

It is important to have a variety in the displays so people will say, "The library certainly has a lot of materials in it. I'll try it out." Displays say, "Here is a sample of something we have in our library. There's a lot more where it comes from." As radio announcers often say, "We have these books and much, much more."

It is important that displays tie in with church events so people will say, "The library is an important part of our church." Such coordination pays rich dividends.

Ideas for displays. Displays require getting fresh, contemporary ideas that will catch the eye of people. Where does one get ideas for displays?

Some evolve from the needs of specific age groups. Preschoolers want pictures to look at. The theme is secondary to the child. He learns of God and His wonderful world, Jesus Christ and His wonderful love, the Bible and its wonderful message, prayer and its wonderful privileges.

Grade schoolers are eager to read for fun; they are eager to learn; they are eager to identify with a hero; they are eager to live right.

Teens need to be encouraged to receive Christ as Saviour; they need to be encouraged to establish daily habits of Bible reading and prayer; they need to be motivated to take a stand for Christ; they need to know how to find God's will for their lives.

Adults have needs for comfort, spiritual strength, family guidance, as well as many more.

Some ideas come from current events. What's happening in the world today? What's happening in your church next week? Is there going to be a missionary conference, an evangelistic meeting, a Sunday School workers' meeting or a women's fellowship meeting?

Displays can tie in by showing books on missionary activities; how to win souls to Christ; how to be a better teacher; or the latest books for women.

Special seasons trigger other good ideas. Displays can be built around the Christmas theme, Easter, a patriotic theme, etc.

Your local Christian bookstore is a fine source for ideas. Look at the displays in the store. They might be centered around new books or best-selling authors. While there, ask on what subjects most books are being sold at the time. These change from year to year.

Ideas may be found in secular stores. Sometimes an idea can be sparked as you go into a department or specialty store. Keep your eyes open for construction, color, materials used in displays and how you might be able to adapt them to your particular need.

From Christian magazines come other ideas. Display ads also can be a source for ideas that could be used in building a display.

A place for displays. Two general areas might be considered for the placing of displays. One is the library. This reaches only people who use the library. The other is any other area of the church property where people gather. Such displays help to reach new people for the library. One disadvantage of a display is that it can pass on its message only to those who pass by. Therefore it is important to place displays where people will see them.

Start by putting a display in the library itself to expose people to more material. A display could be placed on a small table, a low cabinet or even on the bookshelves. A folding shelf extending from a wall also could be utilized.

Inexpensive tables can be made from a barrel, an empty telephone wire reel or various size cardboard boxes. These may be covered with burlap, cloth or colored, corrugated cardboard.

Colorful displays, in addition to giving a message, give the library an aura of life and vitality.

Other areas of the church property to consider: the narthex of the church; a department room of the Sunday School; the fellowship room; near a water fountain; outside the church entrance on a rolling cart.

Planning for displays. Be sure to determine the central theme. Decide on a short, simple message that you want to get over to people.

Then make a preliminary layout. Draw the perimeter of your display area on a sheet of paper. After you complete the following list, sketch in where everything belongs:

Gather books and other materials on the subject of the display. Use the best materials that will help meet needs expressed by the subject.

Props might include display stands, table coverings, signs and objects. These give the books a suitable setting or atmosphere.

The background can be a poster, cloth backdrop or bulletin board. This helps concentrate the focus of a person on the display so they will not be distracted by something behind it. The background also adds to the atmosphere of the display.

It could include an instructional or motivational sign that would help draw attention to the materials on display. Be careful not to make the background too elaborate and thereby distract from the materials displayed.

Use variety. Color has an appealing power to attract attention. To get more color into your display, use crepe paper, colored corrugated cardboard, paint or colored fabric.

Variety in layout also is helpful. Change the way things are placed on the table. Use a variety of angles, heights, combination of books and other materials.

Variety in materials can add to the appeal of the display. Suppose there is a need for family worship helps. Not only could books be displayed, but Bible translations, filmstrips or cassette tapes also could be utilized.

Keep displays orderly. People are turned off by disorderly displays. Watch your displays and if they become disarranged, rearrange them.

Plan simple displays. Do not clutter them by putting too much into each display. Most people like simple things because they can understand them readily.

Have well-lit displays. Use an area that has good overhead lighting. If a spotlight can be directed on the display, this will help draw people.

Keep a card file. On a 4″ × 6″ card, draw a sketch of the display. Indicate the date used, where it was used and any other pertinent information. Another helpful record is to take a Polaroid picture of the display and put it on a card along with the above information.

Either way, by keeping a card on file for each display, ideas can be developed for the future. Also you will be reminded of the themes that have been covered and how they were covered. It will also keep you from repeating themes or display formations too soon.

Evaluate displays, for the sake of improving future display set-ups. After a display has been taken down, ask: "How could it have been made better?" Consider the productivity and effectiveness of each display.

For the sake of improving future display materials, evaluate the materials that have been loaned. Ask the borrowers if the materials met their needs. If not, perhaps you can suggest another book to help them. This also will say to you that you will have to do a better job in selecting topics or materials.

For the sake of improving future patron relations, if borrowers have been helped, try to get them to write on a card—or record on a cassette—a testimonial as to the help they received from the book. Do this while the material is still fresh in their minds. This could be of great help in encouraging other people to use the book.

Change displays. Have a schedule for changing displays. Plan to change displays every one or two weeks, if possible.

Printed Media

The weekly church bulletin. Most pastors control the content of the bulletin. They would be happy to include a few sentences about a book or a certain library service. But someone representing the library must take the responsibility to see that such brief paragraphs are written and given to the person responsible for the typing. A regular use of the bulletin will strengthen people's awareness of your ministry.

Ask the pastor what use the library can make of the bulletin. Prepare copy for two months at a time. Work out delivery details with the one in charge of producing the bulletin so copy can arrive on time.

Be sure copy appeals to all ages with titles that will catch the eye. Give information on a book or a phase of the library ministry in a concise form. Ask for action. You want the reader to do something about the message.

Electronic stencils give the added dimension of an illustration with the copy. Bulletin inserts prepared on colored paper or in an odd shape call attention to the message. Special church bulletins with a cover that could focus on the library, books or reading could be used for Library Sunday.

The monthly church letter. A library column or even a complete page could be included as a part of the church's monthly newsletter. It could tell people the library is a part of the total church ministry.

Keep statistics about the development and use of the library to be used in the letter. Library activities, the purpose of the library, its objectives, the thrust for the coming month, book reviews, book lists for special interests, new book titles and services—all are pertinent subjects for the newsletter.

Layout should include a heading to catch the eye; illustration(s) to give life to the page; information that will be interesting to the reader.

A special insert could be put into the newsletter on a different color paper giving the same information.

Library news sheet. If news of the library cannot be included in the monthly church letter, the library could prepare its own news sheet.

Determine the frequency of the publication—monthly or quarterly. News should include items about new books, gifts received, displays and where they will be, book week plans, circulation figures, tools of the library, testimonials, library needs.

A special news sheet heading should be used each time the paper is sent out that will identify the sheet as a library publication. Develop a distinctive name. If possible have the heading printed even if the rest is mimeographed.

The news sheet should be well planned. It should feature distinctive paragraphs; an uncrowded look; series of articles; descriptive information; interesting and helpful articles. Include information for the whole family and all areas of the church. Speak to the needs, interests and concerns of readers.

Special dodgers. When you have a particular theme to emphasize or you want to give special help along a certain line, consider using special dodgers. A dodger is a one-page sheet measuring anywhere from $4'' \times 5''$ to $6'' \times 8\frac{1}{2}''$.

Mimeograph or have printed two or more on one larger sheet of paper. Use bright colored paper and cut to size. Insert in the church bulletin; distribute to all leaving Sunday School or a morning service.

Be sure your copy zeros in on something particular: a special age group; women's or men's interests; camp; Vacation Bible School; special books, etc.

Layout should include a heading that will give people a desire to read the copy; a simple illustration; a message that highlights a specific library thrust; a challenge to do something about the message; the library name.

For increased effectiveness, use odd sizes—long, narrow strips; short, wide pieces. Provide a quarterly correlated teaching aids' dodger. This requires someone to go over the Sunday School teachers' manuals before the quarter begins.

Find out what supplementary materials are recommended. Check the library's resources to see which of these are in the library. Also check for materials that are in the library, have not been recommended, but correlate.

Provide a list by department showing teachers what they can expect to find in the library that will be of help to them in their teaching ministry for the quarter. Because of the limited quantity for each department, it would be less expensive to photostat the master copy.

Bibliography on certain subjects would be helpful. A list of books including the name of the author and classification number might encourage people to do in-depth study on a given topic.

Bookmarks can be printed or mimeographed. They can be used in departmental distribution or put in books when checked out of the library.

Copy simply should remind readers of the library ministry, services, policies.

Layout might include a symbol that represents the library or its ministry; a simple listing of the information to be made known; the name of the library—possibly the location, if needed.

Your local Christian bookstore has catalogs on bookmarks that can be specially printed to promote the library. These could be used for an anniversary celebration.

Book advertising. Place a ruled piece of paper in a book. At the top write, "The following have read this book and liked it." Have a place for satisfied readers to sign their names. Or the heading might read, "If you have read this book, you will like. . . ." List a few titles of similar books.

Publishers' brochures. Ask your local Christian bookstore to let you know when colorful brochures come in that could be of help in library promotion by stimulating general reading of books.

Plan, chart what you want to do with printed media. Prepare good copy. Ask with regard to each book or audiovisual: Who could use it?

Why would they use it? How can I make it appealing to them?

Prepare a good layout. The headline is worth at least half the ad. A headline can do several things:

It can make a suggestion: "A MUST for Sunday School teachers"; "NEW BOOKS in the church library"; "RECOMMENDED on the radio."

A headline can ask a question: "Looking for a book on. . . . ?" "Want a book to explain. . . . ?" "Have a discipline problem?" "Soul winning, can you do it?"

A good headline also might express a command: "USE audiovisuals in your class"; "Don't be without. . . . !"

Or it might give news: "JUST OFF the press!" "FREE!" "NOW in a handy paperback!" "NO MATTER your age, you can find a book to enjoy."

List specific information about the item. Show the benefit it will be to the users. A simple illustration will enhance the copy. Use the signature—library name and logo—if you have one. If one is not available, spend some time planning a special logo that you can put on stationery, bookmarks, bookplates, etc.

To set off the whole advertisement, use a border. Don't crowd so much copy into an ad that very little white space from the pages will show through.

Other Audiovisual Media

Talks. Have staff members give short book reviews or tell about the library. They could go to:

Sunday School departments and invite individuals and classes to use the library; youth groups and challenge them to read; women's groups and give book reviews.

Also, they could go to any Christian education organization and give library instruction; midweek service and lay prayer requests for the library before the people; Sunday School workers' meetings and tell of the helps that are available for workers.

Many Sunday Schools have a missionary Sunday once a month. Why not a library Sunday once a quarter?

Titles for talks might include the following: "A Minute for Your Mind" (a brief thought from a book); "A Three-Minute Look at a

300-minute Adventure'' (a Christian fiction or biography book review); "The Open Page" (read or summarize a chapter of a book); "Lessons from the Library" (how-to ideas from a book); "Tips from Outstanding Bible Teachers" (seed thoughts from three or four books); "Library Instruction" (how to use the library).

Telephone calls. Find out the subjects, titles and authors of books in which people are interested. Call them when the books come in and say, "We have just received a book in which I think you would be interested." People really will appreciate this concern.

Slides. Take slides of your library that describe the services and show people in action. Slide sequences could include: opening the library door; checking the card catalog; noting shelf labels; sitting at the table reading or studying; checking out a book; children in the library; satellite libraries; the outreach of the library.

If you do not have a library, take slides of some other church library which will show the possibilities of the ministry.

Tapes. Produce a three-minute cassette tape that could be sent to a Sunday School department with a book encouraging people to read.

Prepare a tape to be used in connection with a display. Have a cassette player and earphones with the display. Either buy a prepared tape about a book or make your own. For example, your own tape might run like this:

Ask the listener to: "turn to the title page"—say a word about the author; "turn to the index"—give a few sentences about the key chapters; "turn to a certain page"—point out a very interesting paragraph.

Signs might be used anywhere on the church property directing people to the library. Signs just outside the library should identify the room and give hours.

Interview. Instead of a short talk on a book or the library ministry, have someone interview the librarian, a member of the library staff, a reader, someone representing the character in a book or a visiting author.

Puppets. Have the puppets talk about the library and its services. The librarian can be represented by a puppet taking patrons through the library.

Bulletin boards. Each month put library information in outline form on a sheet of poster board 16 inches × 20 inches. Change color of the poster board monthly but keep same headings; e.g., "Library Profiles."

(See in chapter 11, Vertical file, p. 160.)

Overhead projector. Make a B.A.R. transparency: a sketch to represent the *book* cover; the *author's* name and credentials; the *reasons* why the book was written.

Anyone artistic in your church? Have them illustrate some point made in the book.

Set the overhead in a heavily trafficked area and leave projector on displaying a message via miniature posters while the people pass by. If an ad is large enough, use it to make a transparency. Illustrate library procedures.

Charts. You can make good use of graphs showing budget needs; posters to show layout of the room; illustrations of library policies.

11
Non-book
Materials

In its early years, the average church library contained 95 percent books in its inventory of materials. Then a few years ago, progressive librarians began to catch the vision of the possibilities of adding other-than-books to the library. The purpose of the library today is to provide media of all kinds to help communicate truths about the Word of God.

Following is a list presented to give an idea of the scope of other-than-book media. All media are not listed, only those which are used most frequently in Christian education. If your library collection contains only books, consider adding one other medium at a time and thus increase the scope of the library ministry.

Other Printed Materials

Magazines. Denominational, independent Christian periodicals, magazines used by public school teachers.

Vertical file materials. Clippings from magazines, tracts, small pamphlets and bulletins are put in file folders covering many broad subjects or books of the Bible. When clippings are put in the file, indicate the source and the date on the left-hand side or back of the page. Indicate the subject of the material in the upper left-hand corner so it can be returned to its proper place in the file easily.

Catalogs. From Christian schools, Christian bookstores.

Church materials. Printed or mimeographed materials that have been produced for church activities.

Music. Hymn books. Choir music probably will be kept in the choir's library.

Visual Aids

Flannelgraphs. Bible and Christian application stories, missionary lessons, object lessons. Accessories: Backgrounds, boards and easels.

Filmstrips. 35mm, split 35mm and Show'N'Tell strips. Correlated materials: records, tapes, guides. Accessories: Projectors, screens, previewers.

Flat pictures. Prints, photos, picture rolls. Prints will stay in better condition if they are mounted on poster board and sprayed with a protective plastic coating. Accessories: Picture holder or picture rails.

Maps. Classroom, individual, sets of maps, globes. Classroom maps should also be mounted and sprayed.

Transparencies. Commercially prepared transparencies, handmade transparencies, printed masters. Accessories: Projectors, screen, roller attachment.

Flash cards. Missions, Christian living, salvation.

Charts. Bible, church, special activities. Usually individually made by someone in the church.

Objects, curios, models. illustrating life in Bible times; illustrating life on the mission fields in which the church has an interest.

Puppets. People, animals.

Audio Aids

Disc recordings: music or speaking. Accessories: Portable record player.

Cassettes: sermons, interviews, Bible texts, Bible stories, teacher training. Accessories: cassette player/recorder.

Supplies for Teachers
Suede backed paper, flannel; blank cassettes, tape cleaner; chalk, erasers;

construction paper, poster board; paste, glues; sets of lettering for tracing, etc.; lens cleaner, cloth to wipe lenses; lamps for projectors; crayons, marking pens.

Need for Printed Materials

Magazines. To give insight into what is going on in the Christian world. Concise, pertinent articles on current subjects.

Vertical file. To store valuable materials that otherwise might be thrown away. An inexpensive way to cover many subjects in depth from different viewpoints.

Catalogs. To help young people in their decision-making when considering a Bible institute or college. To help people who cannot get to a Christian bookstore and are in need of materials.

Church materials. To build an interesting history of the church.

Music. To help those who are homebound. Piano and/or organ music is recorded from the hymnal on cassette tapes. The hymnal tapes and player are loaned.

Need for Visual Aids

In general, the use of audiovisuals will result in: a greater retention of what is being taught; a greater understanding of what is being taught; a greater attention to what is being taught.

They should be made available to: uninformed teachers—those who do not know much about audiovisuals and what the materials can do for them; uninstructed teachers—those who do not know how to use audiovisuals and need someone to help them in learning how to make the best use of them.

Flannelgraphs. Valuable in working with children through at least 15 years of age.

Filmstrips. Valuable to use with almost all ages plus workers' training classes of all kinds.

Flat pictures. Valuable for teaching at all age levels. "One picture is worth a thousand words."

Maps. Valuable when teaching the Bible, missions.

Transparencies. Valuable in communicating Bible truths at any age.

Flash cards. Valuable in stressing specific subjects at most age levels.

Charts. Valuable with teens and adults to visualize chronological events.

Objects, curios, models. Valuable to help students get the correct initial impression of a certain item.

Puppets. Valuable to teach children Bible and Christian living truths.

Need for Audio Aids

Disc recordings. Valuable for those who enjoy listening to Christian music of all kinds.

Cassette tapes. Valuable for individual Bible study, teacher training, Christian living helps.

Need for Supplies

Supplies would become part of the library ministry only if the church were underwriting the cost of them, or if the Sunday School superintendent or head of another Christian education organization recommended them as necessary.

Valuable for teachers who cannot get to a bookstore to buy supplies. They can pick up what is needed on the church property.

Valuable for teachers who do not have the money to pay for necessary supplies.

Valuable for teachers who have not prepared fully for Sunday or who forgot to bring from home what they needed for the class.

Valuable to help the church save through controlled buying, united buying and through intra-church use of supplies.

Factors in Your Decision

Certain factors should be taken into consideration before a decision is made (1) to locate non-book materials in the library or (2) to form a separate organization.

Dependent on the present librarian: Is she flexible enough to work with someone who has had experience with audiovisuals? Is she able to understand audiovisuals and their importance? Is she able to organize people, work, details? If the answer is *yes*, keep all media together in one unit. If the answer is "no," look for an assistant who has the sole responsibility for audiovisuals.

Dependent on the vision and enthusiasm of the leadership. Sometimes the book librarian is not enthusiastic, but the audiovisual librarian is very enthusiastic.

It is better to have the audiovisual librarian move ahead rather than be held back by someone without vision and vitality. If both are enthusiastic, they could work together as a powerful team which could be more effective than each one going her own way.

Dependent on space. Sometimes the book library room is so small to begin with that it would be impossible to add audiovisuals in the same room. In this case, the audiovisuals would have to be housed in a different room. However, it should be considered one library, even though located in two rooms.

If possible, keep all media together. In today's public libraries, many other-than-book media are included in the collection. They are stored, shelved and are part of their learning activity centers. The average church library could store, service and effectively loan other-than-book materials, if staff and room are available to handle the expansion.

Book and other media can correlate. Suppose someone needed material on creation. It would be possible to go to the subject cards of the catalog and find there are in the library six books, one flannelgraph story, one filmstrip and a set of transparencies on the subject.

Exposure to other media. People borrowing materials of one medium can be exposed to materials of another medium. A patron may have had no idea that he could find help or enjoyment from another medium until he is exposed to it.

Promotion can be combined. When any of the methods of promotion discussed in the previous chapter are used, audiovisuals can be included.

One library is more impressive. People get the idea the library is a tremendous organization which is of great value to the church.

Criteria for Selection

Authentic. Are the facts actual, accurate and up-to-date?

Suitable. Are the vocabulary and concepts at the user's level?

Vital message. Is there a spiritual challenge?

Interest. Does it interest those who are watching or listening because it has something to do with their everyday living?

Technique. Audio: Is there good tone fidelity? Visual: Are the color and quality of pictures high grade?

Physical features. Is there ease in handling? Is it durable?

Special features. Are there descriptive notes, teachers' or users' guides?

Library potential. Is it flexible for many effective uses by many people?

Selection aids. Have you read recommendations on the item from reliable sources?

Cost. Is it a good dollar value? Will it be economical to keep up? Is it durable?

Displaying Non-book Materials

Other printed media: Place current titles of magazines in tilted shelves or pocket display.

Vertical file requires no actual display space. Selected materials could be mounted on colored construction paper and put on the bulletin board.

Visual aids such as flannelgraphs, flash cards, charts, flat pictures can be placed on easels.

Clippings from filmstrip brochures or catalogs can be mounted on colored construction paper, put on bulletin board.

Objects, models, curios can be used to tie with book displays.

Maps, transparencies can be promoted through listings in a quarterly correlated teaching aids dodger.

Select two or three puppets to display at a time. Use dowel board.

Audio aids. Disc recordings can be displayed and stored in a browser box. Use special holder.

Display cassette tapes with special book title promotion. Use special holder.

Storage

Other printed media: Retain 12 months' supply of each magazine in cabinet. After 12 months, cut up the magazine and put the clippings in the vertical file.

For the vertical file use one or more drawers of a file cabinet. File material according to subject and according to the books of the Bible.

Visual aids: flannelgraph stories: put each story in a brown envelope and file according to subject and/or book of the Bible—place envelopes in a file cabinet. Backgrounds: file in cabinet.

Use filmstrip cabinet.

Flat pictures should be stored in file cabinet.

File picture size maps in file cabinet. Wall: special drawer.

Use a file cabinet for transparencies.

Similarly, for flat cards and charts, use a file cabinet.

Objects, models, curios require the use of a cabinet.

For puppets, use dowel boards in a cabinet.

Audio aids: disc recordings should be stored in a browser box.

Cassette tapes should be stored in a cassette cabinet.

Supplies may be stored in a cabinet or special drawers.

Circulation

In cataloging audiovisuals keep the system as simple as possible. One of the simplest is a symbol/number system. Letter symbols are given to each category of audiovisuals. A symbol is suggested for each audiovisual under "code."

Along with the symbol, assign consecutive numbers under each category as items are entered into the library. The symbol and number constitute the call number. Thus the first filmstrips purchased would be assigned FS1, the second FS2, etc.

Make the necessary records. It is just as important to make an ownership record of audiovisuals as it is books. As much of the following information as possible should be included in the record which should be verified by a yearly inventory. The numbers preceding each item are used under "inventory record" for each audiovisual.

Title: of the audiovisual. Communicator: the person(s) speaking, performing, or the compiler of the item. Accessories: guide, book, record. Number of pieces: to make a complete set. (Must be counted when returned).

Special information: black and white or color; size, time involved, age level, purpose or use. Copyright date. Producer: name of the manufacturer. Purchase date. Cost.

These supplies are needed to keep accurate records when items are

Example of Audiovisual Main Entry Card

```
TR8        The Fruit of the Spirit (Transparency)
              Norma Felske    Scripture Press 1979
              12  prepared transparencies, 4 duplicating
           masters, notes for 10 sessions, for use from
           Jr. Hi through Adults
              8 pages of suggestions for teaching.
              For Bible studies based on John 15 and
           Galations 5:22-23

           1. Holy Spirit    2. John 15    3. Galations 5:22-23

              I. Author
```

borrowed. Listed under "check out materials" for each audiovisual is the location of the first three items:

Booking pockets: a pocket in which the booking card is kept while the item is in the library. Booking cards: to show the staff where an item is when it is not in the library, and when it will be back. Date due slips: to remind users of when the item must be back in the library.

Individual brown kraft envelopes 12 inches × 15½ inches: certain visual aids can be kept in their designated envelope while in the library. The envelope also can be used for patrons to carry the aid after checking it out.

The book pocket with title, call number and the number of pieces is pasted along with the date due slip on the envelope. The booking card with the same information typed on it is put into the pocket.

General brown kraft envelopes 12 inches × 15½ inches: audiovisuals kept in a special piece of equipment can be placed in the envelope for the patron to carry. A book pocket without any information and a date due slip are pasted on the envelope. If there is a booking card for the item, it will have the title and call number typed on it. The cards are filed in a tray until they are ready to be used.

Catalog cards need to be made for audiovisuals. The cards correspond with the title, subject and author cards for books. However, not all audiovisuals need all cards.

Media designation. In order for a patron to quickly see that an item is not a book and be able to tell the kind of audiovisual it is, the card must be marked properly as to what media it is. This designation can be done in several ways:

It can be typed after the title. It can be typed above the call number. A magic marker can be used to line a media color designation at the top edge of the card. Catalog cards can be purchased with colors already on them.

Media designation colors can vary. Put your color code in the library manual and follow it for consistency.

The main entry card. With audiovisuals, this is usually the title card. It is the principal card from which all other entries for the aid are made. The categories of information needed on the card are:

The call number. This number is made up of the media symbol and the media number.

The title statement. The full *title* of the audiovisual as it appears on the box, label, or guide. The *producer* of the audiovisual. The *copyright* date.

The communicator's name(s). The artist, the person(s) speaking, performing, or the compiler of the item.

The description: age designation; technical description; contents of a module, set or kit; any accessory such as a guide, book, or record.

Notes: titles of songs, a description of the audiovisual or an explanation of what is in the item.

The tracings: a record of what other cards have been made in order to find them again.

As the cataloger gathers the above information, she writes it on a work slip. All cards then can be typed by an informed typist saving valuable time for the cataloger.

The subject entry cards. Many people who come into the library will ask for material by subject. Therefore it is important to have a good subject file. Information needed on the card includes:

The call number; the subject heading; the title statement; the communicator's name, edition, and release/publication statement.

The added entry cards. In this case, the author card would be con-

Audiovisual Subject Entry Skeleton Card

```
            SUBJECT HEADING
  Call    Title statement (media designation)
  No.         Communicator's name and edition
          release/publication statement
```

sidered an added entry card. The categories of information that go on this card are the same as on the subject entry card except instead of the subject heading, the author's name would be used at the top of the card and omitted after the title statement.

The main entry card and inventory card should be typed as follows: call number—media symbol and number (3rd line; 2nd space).

Title statement (3rd line; 1st indentation). Title of the audiovisual, period, two spaces, producer, comma, one space, copyright date, period. When continuing the title statement to the next line, begin at the 2nd indentation.

Communicator's name(s)—begin two lines below the end of the title statement: 2nd indentation. If names must continue to the next line, begin it at the 1st indentation.

Description—begin two lines below end of the communicator's names: 2nd indentation. If description must continue to the next line, begin it at the 1st indentation.

Notes—begin the first note two lines below the end of the description statement; 2nd indentation. Each note begins a new paragraph at the 2nd indentation. Lines for each note which are too long and must continue on a second line, begin at the 1st indentation.

Tracings—begin at least three lines below the notes; 1st indentation. Type in capital letters, column form. If necessary, tracings can be continued on the back of the card near the bottom by using the word "over" on the front of the card.

Added entry and subject entry cards. Subject cards should be typed as follows:

Call number: 3rd line; 2nd space.

Subject heading: 1st line; 2nd indentation. Type in capital letters.

Title statement: 3rd line; 1st indentation.

Communicator's name(s): two lines below the title statement; 2nd indentation.

Description: two lines below communicator's names; 2nd indentation.

Notes: two lines below description; 2nd indentation.

Title cards should be typed as follows:

Call number: 3rd line; 2nd space.

Communicator's name: 1st line; 2nd indentation.

Title statement: 3rd line; 1st indentation.

(See in chapter 9, Added entry cards, p. 126.)

Processing Audiovisuals

Other printed media. Magazines require processing as follows:

Code: none; inventory record: none; check out material: use 3″ × 5″ cards to record name of magazine, date of issue, borrower's name, and date due. Stamp the date due on the cover of the magazine. Catalog cards: none; call number location: none.

Vertical file processing consists of: code: none; inventory record: none; check out material: use general envelope in which to put materials. Use 3″ × 5″ card to record number of articles taken and the name of the borrower.

Catalog cards: none. Cards may be put in the catalog under the subjects listed in the vertical file with a reference to the vertical file. Call number location: none.

Visual aids. Flannelgraphs should be processed as follows:

Code: stories = FL; backgrounds = FLB; inventory record: 1, 3, 4 (number of figures, 6, 7, 8, 9); check out materials: on individual envelope; catalog cards: subject and title cards; media color: red. Call number location: upper left-hand corner of envelope and guide book.

Filmstrips should be processed as follows:

Code: filmstrip only = FS; filmstrip with sound: discs = RFS; tape = TFS; inventory record: 1, 2, 3 (record, guide) 4 (number of frames). If set, number of filmstrips, 5 (color/black and white) 6, 7, 8, 9.

Check out materials: general envelope; catalog cards: subject, title; media color: green; call number location: upper left-hand corner of script or manual; at the beginning of the strip, on record label.

Flat pictures require processing as follows:

Code: PI; inventory record: none; check out materials: general envelope; use 3″ × 5″ cards to record name of picture, due date and name of borrower. Catalog cards: none; call number location: none.

Map processing consists of:

Code: individual maps = MA; map sets = MAS; inventory record: 1, 4 (if a set, number of pieces), 5 (size), 6, 7, 8, 9; check out materials: in loaning smaller maps, put in general envelope; catalog cards: subject card only; media color: orange; call number location: on back of map or map mounting.

Transparencies should be processed thusly:

Code: TR; inventory record: 1, 2, 3, 4 (if set), 5 (overlays), 6, 7, 8, 9; check out materials: general envelope; catalog cards: subject, title, author; media color: yellow; call number location: transparency frame; if not mounted, mark with a pen in the lower left-hand corner of transparency.

Flash card processing is as follows:

Code: FC; inventory record: 1, 3, 4 (if loose sheets) 6, 7, 8, 9; check out materials: if in a book form, inside front cover; if separate pictures, individual envelopes.

Catalog cards: subject, title, author; media color: purple; call number location: lower left-hand corner of front cover; individual envelope.

Charts require processing as follows:

Code: CH; inventory record: none; check out materials: use 3″ × 5″ card to record the item, due date and borrower's name. Paste date due slip on back. Catalog cards: subject; media color: purple.

Processing for objects, models, curios follows:

Code: RE (for realia); inventory record: none. Usually these are not

Suggestion for
Audiovisual Reservation Slip

Borrower _____ Card No. _____ Date _____

Department _____ Date desired _____ Time _____

Where equipment is to be delivered _____

Date to be returned _____

Materials needed

Classification number	Title	Media

Equipment needed

Projector _____ Cassette recorder _____

Screen _____ Record player _____

- -
(For Library use only)

Equipment checked _____ Date returned _____

Materials checked _____

Action taken _____

Signed _____

very valuable in dollars and cents. Check out materials: use $3'' \times 5''$ card to record the item, due date and borrower's name.

Catalog cards: subject only; media color: brown; call number location: if possible place in inconspicuous place with permanent ink.

Puppets require this processing:

Code: PU; inventory record: 5 (size, kind; i.e., person, animal, type of action), 6, 7, 8, 9; check out materials: place puppet in a box such as a shoe box. (Excellent boxes can be purchased at the post office.) If possible place materials on inside of lid.

Catalog cards: subject card; media color: black; call number location: inconspicuous place with permanent ink.

Learning games and puzzles should be processed in this manner:

Code: LPG; inventory record: 1, 4 (number of pieces), 5 (size of completed puzzle, age-level, purpose or use), 6, 7, 8, 9; check out materials: general envelope.

Catalog cards: subject card; media color: blue; call number location: on bottom of the box or back or puzzle frame.

Audio aids require this kind of processing:

Records and tapes: code: disc recording = RD; cassette or reel-to-reel tape = RT; inventory record: 1, 2, 3, 4 (if set of tapes), 5 (time), 6, 7, 8, 9; check out materials: discs—back of jacket; cassettes—card cut to fit in box.

Catalog cards: subject, title, author, speaker or artist: media color: pink; call number location: discs—jacket, record label; cassettes—tape label and box.

Equipment for Audiovisuals

Inventory record. Each piece of equipment should carry an item number. This can be applied with a plastic label, self-adhesive label, an etching on the item, or marked with a permanent pen.

The item number, description of the item, serial number, manufacturer and accessories that go with the basic item should be put into the record book.

Check out materials. Use an audiovisual checkout card for each item. Equipment should be checked out only by those who know how to operate it.

12
Enlarging
Your Ministry

The possibilities of ministry for your church library are unlimited. The suggestions given here are only a few to whet your appetite. They are presented to challenge librarians who direct a library that has a good administrative foundation and is functioning efficiently to go on to further service within and outside the church.

A ministry is possible to young children and adults, as well as to all who are in between, to the believer and nonbeliever. A ministry is possible in cooperating with other groups in the church, initiated by the library expressing its objectives.

Think of the possibilities of your library ministry as if you were taking a long trip by car. You are making your way to a great mountain chain. Soon you will come to the beautiful green rolling foothills. In the next few hours, you will enjoy the view a hundred miles away where the hills are much larger. But in the days ahead, you will see great mountain peaks. Undoubtedly there will be many areas you will not be able to see.

Today you are enjoying the library ministry God has given you. It may seem very small to you and yet God is making it a blessing to the people of your church. As you work to develop the library year by year, as you adopt some of the suggestions to your particular situation, you will find your library ministry climbing to new heights.

The suggestions you encounter may seem to be a great insurmountable mountain of ideas. But they need be done only one at a time. Some of them you may be doing already. Others you may have the privilege of doing in another year. Still others may be enjoyed only by those who follow and build on what you have done.

Some suggestions may not fit into your particular situation at all. But you may gain a vision of what can be done through your library and keep on working and building. Much remains to be accomplished and enjoyed.

One reason so many possibilities exist is that so many resources are available. Only those who have attended a convention of the Christian Booksellers Association have any idea as to the great wealth of materials God has provided for His people today. Hundreds of suppliers display their materials for Christian bookstores, using the largest convention centers in the country because of the vast amount they have to show.

From the thousands of items displayed, your local Christian bookstore buyer must select those materials which he feels will meet the needs of the people and their ministries in the area he serves. It would be impossible for him to stock every book, audiovisual or supply that is displayed.

From the selected stock of items displayed in your local Christian bookstore, the librarian must make intelligent decisions and buy those resources she feels will most help the people of her church.

Developing Readers to Enjoy the Ministry

Most librarians are concerned about collecting, storing and circulating books to the few who seem responsible. But part of your concern should be to get more readers to enjoy and be helped by Christian literature. How can you find new readers?

Recognize the kinds of readers in your church. Some are avid readers—those who want to read, like to read many kinds of books, and will sacrifice time and money to read. Very little work is required in getting these people into the library.

Some are casual readers—those who read books mainly for pleasure and fun. They read Christian fiction and sometimes may go to Christian biography. Or perhaps they may read books on certain subjects if they are written superficially or from an experiential standpoint. You need to whet the appetites of these people to go beyond this into more in-depth books.

Some are inexperienced readers—those who read slowly and perhaps with difficulty. They need much encouragement and need to be helped in finding the right kinds of books for their need.

Still others are self-improvement readers—those who want to increase their knowledge in a certain area of Bible truth. They find and read material for a course or to do research work, or they are doing independent Bible study. They read to gain supplementary information on what is being taught.

Self-improvement readers also may be those who want to improve their Christian service. They may involve a Sunday School teacher, committee member, usher, etc. You need to let self-improvement readers know what is available for their use and prepare interesting book lists.

It is important to be sensitive to the reading needs of the entire church family.

Remember the Needs of Readers

Preschool "readers" (up to 5 years of age) need visualized books and audiovisuals to help them understand Bible concepts. No child is too young for a picture book. The theme is secondary to the child.

They need the story to reflect their everyday world—mother, father, house, pets, things they do, familiar animals. They need to be read to—over and over. They like to hear the rhythm of the words. They need parental help to get books.

Early grade school readers (ages 5-9) need picture books and easy books as they begin to read. Interest often runs ahead of ability to read. They like stories about family life, school days, children, grown-ups, animals, space, travel, rockets, jets, airplanes, cars, fire engines, machines at work, policemen, doctors, nurses, mailmen, bus drivers.

Children at this age can become very avid readers.

Older grade school readers (ages 9-12) need specialized interest books. They like books which deal with mysteries, sports, adventures, history, fiction, strange places, lives of real people, animals, humor, fun with words, riddles, limericks, information, encyclopedias, fantasy.

Teenagers need to develop reading habits before they leave high school, otherwise it is very doubtful if they will later. Teens reach back for books of the older grade school readers and reach forward for adult books.

They like resource books, romance, adventure, mystery, biography, science, animals, sports. They need books that will help develop their Christian lives, leadership abilities, Bible study needs.

Older teens also need books on career guidance. Provide books that are an introduction, not a barrier, to adult reading. Teenagers can become very lax in their reading. They need encouragement to fit reading into their schedule of life.

Young adults need help with marriage, the home, finances and a variety of spiritual problems. They need personal development books; books on faith and doctrine.

Mature adults need material that will help them with Christian living, bring comfort, explain doctrine and help with an in-depth study of God's Word. They need inspiration for daily living; help with problems relating to health, loss of loved one, loneliness, boredom, inability to accept change.

If a child is to read, the parent must read. If a child sees that his parents enjoy reading, it will help him to see he is missing something important for his life.

In choosing books for the various age levels, the selector should consider the:

Relevancy of the book. A book that is relevant will lead an individual in an understanding of the facts of the Word of God and then show how these facts apply to his everyday life.

Reading interests. Become acquainted with the people of the church in order to ascertain their needs. Through contacts with teachers, try to get information about reading interests of students. The areas in which people live, such as rural, urban, suburban, make a difference in reading habits.

Reading differences. Not only are there differences in the reading characteristics of children and youth, but you must also recognize the differences between men and women. Women read more fiction than men. Men tend to read more on applying Christianity to everyday life. Women do more recreational reading. Men do more work-related reading.

Special Environment

All readers are not found in normal home situations. There are many whose day could be brightened, whose life could be lifted, through Christian literature.

Homebound. The library can have a ministry to the handicapped. In America today, approximately one out of seven people have a permanent physical disability. It may be either from a birth defect, a disease, an accident, a wound, or advanced age.

Many cannot leave the confines of their homes. A special home delivery service for shut-ins could help them to enjoy books and other media. Utilize young people to be carriers for this service.

If someone goes around the church property by wheelchair, can he get into your library? He may be visually limited. Have you put into your collection large-type books and cassettes that can be used by such people?

If a member or friend of your church finds himself in a cast, does the library seek to minister to that one? To the boy or girl with a children's disease; the youth recuperating from an accident; the adult recovering from surgery? To those who because of age do not have the strength to get to church; those caring for the homebound; the mother caring for a sick child; the adult caring for a convalescent?

Institution bound. Is your library ministering to those in hospitals, while they wait—before or after an operation? In nursing/convalescent homes (books for those who can read or can be read to—cassettes for inspirational music or messages)?

Are you reaching the armed forces, with books for a chapel library? Children in detention homes? Books for a prison library?

Developing Those Who Are Non-readers

You have been considering people who read, who can be induced to read or who can be read to. Nonreaders need to be sold on reading. Why is it that so many people do not read?

Lack of training. Forty million people in the United States are unable to read. One tenth of the population has less than fourth-grade reading ability. Those who cannot read well enough to read a newspaper or a personal shopping list are called functional illiterates. Some people read very poorly and, because it is so difficult, make no effort to get books from the library.

Missionaries go to other countries to help nationals learn to read so they will be able to read the Bible and other books. But who takes time to help people in our own country or our own church to learn to read in order for them to be blessed by reading the Word of God and Christian books?

Lack of time. Many people have two jobs. Others are busy with church work. You need to set before people the necessity of getting spiritual input through reading books. You must motivate people to make a small daily investment in reading because of the dividends it will pay in their lives now and for eternity.

Encourage people to take advantage of: waiting time—in the doctor's office, airport, etc.; vacation time—while traveling in a plane, resting in the motel, etc.; coffee time—a Christian book and a cup of coffee can go very well together; quiet time—a few minutes with the Bible and a book before they go to sleep.

Lack of education. The higher the level of education, the more reading is done. Provide easy reading books and promote their use to these people.

Lack of priority. Other things come first, such as TV, radio, sports and trips. These people can read if they really want to. But they say, "I haven't time to read."

If such people would read 15 minutes a day, they would read ½ a book a week; 2 books a month; 20 books a year or 1,000 books in a lifetime. Someone has estimated that this would be equal to going through college five times.

List the average time to read a book. You may estimate the reading time of a certain book to be one minute per page. Provide a small slip of paper for selected books. Title it, "It's Easy to Read This Book."

Let's say a person can give only five minutes a day to reading. Show for the first day to read chapter 1 (approximately five pages, five minutes to read). Show for the second day, to read chapters 2 and 3 (only about three pages each).

Lack of understanding. Some people are not able to read the English language. If you have those in your church who read better in another language, you should consider their need for books and cassettes.

Look for Readers Outside the Church

Church prospects. Those who are being visited or those who have visited the church need to be told that the church has an important library ministry.

Satellite libraries. Set up a satellite library in an apartment complex or housing project.

Mobile library. The church bus could be used during the week as a mobile library to go to different neighborhoods with books to be loaned, read stories or even show a filmstrip.

Missionaries. Books could be sent to the church missionary family.

Reaching Readers for the Ministry

Personal contacts. Welcome people who come into the library. This friendly touch will help to keep them coming. Greet people of the church who do not come into the library. Pleasantly remind them of the ministry.

Ask each member of the staff to make personal contacts. Remind them that there must be a real caring for people. Provide individual reading guidance.

Organizational contacts. Keep in touch with Sunday School teachers at all age levels. Encourage teachers to bring their classes into the library once a year as part of their regular class period. Offer book reviews for men's and women's organizations.

Offer to discuss children's reading at an adult Sunday School social. Prepare a special exhibit of books for a Sunday School parent-teacher's night. Have a two-generation display of books. Use books parents owned and read as children along with current children's books.

Printed page contacts. Wherever you can, tie in with an existing publication of the church or one of its organizations.

(See in chapter 10, Printed Media, p. 148.)

Special project contacts. Library card promotion (see chapter 3). Library open house: at the start of the library and at each anniversary date, invite everyone to come to the library for "Tour, Tea and Talk." They are shown around the library, offered tea (coffee or milk) and encouraged to ask questions.

Library week: prepare a schedule and invite people to come in for

"Fifteen Minutes with Your Library." Give a short course on basic library skills.

"Plus Time." Encourage people to come into the library before or after a service to read from a selected chapter of a book or listen to a ten-minute tape that deals with the subject of the message. Provide paper and pencil for note taking. A tape provided by the pastor could be very effective.

The church auditorium. Announcements from the pulpit. The person who often gets the best results is the pastor. Another member of the pastoral staff or the librarian also could make announcements.

Church bulletin (see in chapter 10, Printed Media, p. 148). Dedication of workers: to be done yearly in an evening service. Testimonials: if God has spoken to someone through a book, it would make a good testimony in a Sunday or midweek service.

The church narthex. Display books and other materials that will tie in with the message of the day. Books can give in-depth consideration to the subject being presented. Tapes also can give correlated materials or a repetition of what was given.

Sunday School department room. Maintain small satellite libraries in various departments. Appoint someone in the department to care for it. Change books every other week.

The main library provides promotion, watches the condition of the books, charges books, follows up on overdue books, etc.

The library room. Encourage people to discover what quietness can do for their studying. Use of the library during Sunday School, Children's Church.

Welcome letter. All new members are sent a letter from the librarian telling of the library services along with a family application form for a library card. (See chapter 3).

Short talks. Teaser talks: take books to groups. Read from a book and stop at an interesting place. The book must be borrowed to find out what follows. Library Sunday. Use a staff member to go into a department and in an interesting way give a library report.

Pupil participation. If there is room, encourage people to bring items they have created into the library to be displayed. Such items as pictures, handcraft, posters, and models could be used.

Children's outreach. Story hour: after school, on Saturdays, or during the summer, books can be read to children in the library. Not only will the child get the message of the book, but it also may inspire them to read for themselves.

• Film/filmstrip program: a series of four to six weeks showing Bible stories, Christian fiction stories from the library collection. Youth day: give older teens the responsibility for a day of being a librarian or one of the staff members of the library. Work in cooperation with the high school teachers and youth sponsor.

• Children's book club: enroll children of the same age group in a club whose goal is to read a book a month. Books are chosen from a list the library committee has prepared.

After a book is read, a report of a paragraph or two should be written on why the reader liked the book. Then the report should be posted on a bulletin board or put with a display. Those who read 12 books or more, and make reports, should be recognized during a special church service.

Home library development: help build libraries in homes that fit the needs of the home. Work with family members to determine the thrust of their library. Offer to pick up books for people when you go to the bookstore.

• Prepare a monthly reading calendar in which books would be suggested that could be purchased for the following types of home libraries:

• Worker's library: books that give how-to for a Sunday School teacher, superintendent, organizational worker, children's church worship leader.

• Children/youth library: books for the children of the home.

• Parent's library: books that will help parents in their task of bringing up their children.

• Enjoyment library: books on Christian fiction, biographies, etc.

• Student's library: provide a list of basic Bible study books. Keep the list current.

Author's visit: arrange to honor an author. When people hear an author, they will be more apt to read his writings.

Enrichment tables: make these available whenever meetings are going on that center around missions, evangelism, Bible study, etc.

Christian Education Emphasis

Help teachers in planning a work assignment for students that involves research.

Advise teachers quarterly what is available for their use in the next quarter. (See in chapter 10, Special dodgers, p. 149.)

Orient new teachers. At the beginning of each school year, have an informal workshop for the new workers to acquaint them with the kinds of books the library has as well as the use of audiovisuals and equipment.

(Work closely with teachers through the quarter in helping them find materials that will enrich their teaching program through the use of varied printed matter and audiovisuals.)

Ask that materials be brought to the library or if there is a satellite in the room, take it there. This material will be used to obtain clippings for the vertical file and pictures.

Audiovisual workshop. Teach workers to operate audiovisual equipment.

Providing Books for Readers

The following is a subject list of books which should be kept in mind by a growing library. It is given to:

Show the range of subjects. Of course these are not all the subjects, but they are basic subjects with which every librarian should be acquainted. She should be familiar with the term as well as know the meaning of the term. The subjects listed are not necessarily subject headings. (See chapter 8 for information on subject headings.)

Suggest a general location for the subjects in the Dewey Classification System. No attempt has been made to put all the subjects in the 200 class. Church librarians today need to learn to make use of other classes.

Specific titles under each subject were purposely not given. It would be impossible to give a complete and current list of books. When you need books on a specific subject, go to your local Christian bookstore and ask them to show you the books they carry relating to the subject. In fact, if they have some background on your church, they would probably be glad to make a recommendation as to the best books for your particular church library.

Age-level books
  Practicing Christian living
    Children   248.82
    Teens   248.83
    Adults   248.84
  Teaching
    Children   268.432
    Teens   268.433
    Adults   268.434
  Psychology
    Children   155.4
    Teens   155.5
    Adults   155.6

Bibles
  Modern versions   220.5

Bible commentaries (On every book of the Bible to give fuller meaning to passages of Scripture and how to apply the Word of God to life.)
  Old Testament books   221–224
  New Testament books   225–228
  The Bible as a whole   220.7

Bible reference books (usually on the reserve shelf)
  Concordances (to help find location of verses) 220.2
  Dictionaries, encyclopedias   220.3
  Atlas (visual history of Bible events)   220.9

Bible resource books (in-depth reservoirs for understanding the Bible)
  Archaeology (point out the accuracy of
    the Bible)   220.93
  Manners and customs (how people lived,
    dressed, worked)   220.91
  Theology in general   201.1
  Origin and authority of the Bible 220.1

Christian education
  Administration   268.1
  Child psychology   155.4
  Pedagogy   268.4
  Teacher training   268.6

Teaching aids	268.6
Youth leaders	268.3
Church	250–280
Administration	254
Contemporary	261
Doctrine	262
History	270
Programs	264
Contemporary social issues	
Abortion	179.7
Depression	616.89
Divorce	301.4284
Drugs	178
Homosexuality	301.4157
Mental health	131
Women's rights	301.412
Doctrinal books (emphasizing the doctrinal position of your church)	230–240
Bibliology—Bible	220
Theology—God	231
Pneumatology—Holy Spirit	231.3
Christology—Jesus Christ	232
Anthropology—Man	233
Soteriology—Salvation	234
Eschatology—Last things	236
Ecclesiology—Church	262
Apologetics	239
Evangelism	269
Family and home	
Sex	301.418
Marriage	301.42
Parent-child relationships	649
Family finances	640.42
Family devotions	249
General reading	
Ethics	170

Motivation	152.5
Physical fitness	613.7
Poetry	808.81
Senior citizens	301.435
Singles	155.642

Inspirational books

Biographies (for special categories see chapter 8)	920 or B
Christian living	248
Comfort	242.4
Daily devotions	242.2
Death, dying	236.1
Pain, suffering	242.4

Languages

Greek	480
Hebrew	492.4
Spanish	460

| *Missions* | 266 |

Recreation

Fiction	F
Game books	790
Handicrafts	745.5
Humorous books	808.87

Religions, cults	290–295
Astrology	133.5
Demonology	235
Science and the Bible	215

Special days

| Christmas | 232.1 |
| Easter | 232.5 |

13
Time
to Evaluate

Every library committee should take a good look at its library on a regular basis. Unless a library staff looks at itself objectively, church libraries will not develop as they should.

Evaluation should take place not less than every six months. At this time, committee members must think through carefully every detail of the library operation. Each step must justify itself. For each operation ask: Is it necessary? Can it be improved? Can it be done more easily or more effectively in some other way?

Many advantages are gained by evaluation. It keeps the whole library program in view. No areas will be overlooked. Evaluation also motivates the committee to develop areas not in operation. A lack in one area may affect the rest of the library ministry. It enables the committee to strengthen the areas now in operation and thus make them more productive.

Administration

Without proper administration, time, effort and money will be lost.

Planning. Do we have a *plan* for future development in writing? Do we know *where* we want to go? Do we spend part of our library committee time in *planning* for the future? What do we *anticipate* the growth of the church will be in the next five years? Is it growing rapidly, steadily or not at all? How will this affect the library ministry?

Prepare a *five-year plan* as to what you expect the library to be and do. *List your goals* for the various areas shown in this evaluation chapter.

Reporting. Do we *gather* information and make accurate *records* of all activities to be used in making reports? Are we *consistently reporting* to the leadership and membership of the church what the library is doing?

Prepare a *monthly report* to the church board and/or the Christian Education Committee. Prepare an *end-of-the-year* report that can be presented with the rest of the reports at the annual meeting of the church.

Organization. In what areas of our library is more *organization* needed? Are the *rules* of the library being followed? Is the library *open* when it is needed?

Make a yearly distribution of the *rules of the library* to the entire congregation. Prepare a *monthly schedule* for workers. In this way each staff member will know exactly what is required of her and you will be able to have a maximum of times when the library is open.

(See chapter 3, Administration.)

Media

Without sufficient media, activity in the library will be minimized. Are the materials in the library meeting the *needs* of the people of the church? Can people *find* materials on subjects in which they are interested?

Are there materials that are *not being used*? Why? Are they useful? Are the materials being properly *prepared* for circulation to get maximum use from them?

List all the age levels and determine if you have a minimum of *10 books* for each. Review your procedures for *preparing materials* for circulation with the idea of improving it so materials will last longer.

Book media. Of the books that have recently been purchased, how have they been *received*? What is the *condition* of the books in the collection? Are the books being *prayerfully* and *carefully* selected? Can a good *reason* be given for each book being in the library?

When selecting, *ask* about each book, "Who can use it?" Prepare a *selection policy.* (See chapter 7.)

Other-than-book media. Can the media be *correlated* with the teaching ministry of the church? Is there *hardware* as well as *software* for a practical use of the audiovisuals?

Make a special effort each fall to *orient teachers* in the use of audiovisuals. Check over hardware and software to make sure they are in usable condition and that replacement *lamps* for projectors are on hand.

New Media. What is being done to make the *library committee* aware of new materials? How many new materials have been added in the last three months?

Assign different staff members to find out what new media is available and what people would like to see in the library. *Assign* someone to go to the bookstore, another to read magazines and brochures for ideas, others to talk to adults, youth, children and teachers.

(See chapter 7, Selection, p. 99; chapter 11, Non-book Materials, p. 155.)

Service

Without service, a library will not be successful even though it has the best administration and media. What happens when someone comes to the library and says, "Can you help me?"

When people come to the library, can they get what they *want*, get the next available item to it, or do many go away empty-handed? Is it easy to *locate* materials in the library? Are we successful in determining the *needs* of the people of the church?

How will you get people to *understand* and *appreciate* the library ministry? How can you make the library ministry *personal* so people will feel they have a need for it? Is there a *"caring"* for people by the service that is given? Does the staff enjoy helping others? Are they service-minded?

List at least three ways in which you can *minister* to individuals through the library ministry. List ways in which you can determine the *tastes* and *interests* of those coming into the library.

(See in chapter 1, Service Ministry, p. 18.)

Staff

Without enough workers, the library cannot function effectively, circulate media or perform the services it should.

Are there *enough* people to get the work done? Is the staff able to *keep up* with their work? Do the members of the staff *understand* what they are to do? Does the staff have the *ability* to answer questions of those who come into the library? Do the people who come into the library feel the staff is competent?

Has the staff had any *training* for their ministry? Are they being trained as you expect Sunday School teachers to be trained? Do the members of the staff have an outgoing *personality?* Are they courteous, well-groomed, friendly and have a smile? Is the staff *recruited* as other Christian education personnel are recruited?

List the *jobs* that need to be done. Show which ones are being done. Put jobs to be filled on prayer lists and contact lists. *Describe* what is to be done for each job in the library so those who are doing the job or who will do the job will know what is expected of them. Indicate library how-to books they should read for their job.

Ask the staff: In what areas of answering questions do you feel need of help? _____Where to find materials_____What to use_____What to read. Write in 50 words or more what you feel the library is trying to do. What is your vision of the library ministry? What is the library all about? State briefly why you are working in the library.

List at least three people who might be *possibilities* to help in the library. Hold regular *staff meetings* for: training, to advise of new materials, and to explain ways in which the materials can be used.

(See in chapter 3, People, p. 37.)

Finances

Without money, plans could not come to fulfillment and media could not be purchased.

Have you prepared a *yearly budget*? Do you follow the budget? What are you doing to *motivate* individuals to give? What effort has been made to *enlist* financial help from other organizations in the church?

If you were not working in the library, would you make a *contribution* to it because of the service they perform for you? What has the library done that it might deserve to be better *supported* by the church?

What contacts do you have with *families* to get their cooperation? Are you careful to *acknowledge* and *record* every gift that has been given to the library?

Prepare a yearly budget showing anticipated expenses and income. Write out *reasons* why organizations and individuals should support the library financially.

(See chapter 4, "Finances.")

Housing

The room in which the library is located can be a stigma or a stimulation to the library ministry.

What are the *advantages* of your library location and room? What are the *disadvantages*? Is the *decor* of the room inviting and comfortable?

Make a layout of the *church property* with the library as the focal point. Analyze the location of the library for its centrality and place in the line of traffic.

Analyze *the room you now use* for the way the space is being used. Is it to the best of its potential? List ways you could improve the use of the room. Can it be rearranged to get more efficient use of the space?

Ask five or more people to give you their *reaction* to your library room—the decor, the layout, the location, the service. Ask people of various ages, those who are in different organizations as well as the leadership and general membership.

Equipment

Without the proper equipment, organization of materials is very difficult.

Do you have open, adjustable *shelving* for books? Is the *service desk* adequate to provide all the services necessary for such an area? Is the *card catalog cabinet* available and sufficient to handle the necessary books?

List the equipment you need, along with a plan to get finances to buy it.

(See chapter 5, Housing and Equipment, p. 67.)

Promotion

Unless people are motivated to use the library, much of the collection with all the work involved is wasted.

Have you planned a *consistent promotion* of the library for at least six months ahead? Are you displaying books in areas outside the library to motivate people who do not come into the library? Are you cooperating in the major thrusts of the church for the next year?

Determine what you can do to let the peole of the church *know weekly* what the ministry of the library is. Analyze what has been the *result* of any publicity you have done. Should certain types be continued or changed?

List three possible *places* on the church property you could put a display. List five things you would like to *emphasize* about the library ministry to your church.

(See chapter 10, Promotion, p. 135.)

Weekly Circulation

Good circulation is the result of a good evaluation of the above items followed by action.

Is the circulation of materials *increasing* or *decreasing*? Why is this? What *percentage* of your books are moving? Are people not coming into the library because of something you are *failing* to provide? Are materials being *returned* on time? If not, is it because of lack of information or lack of enforcement of policies?

List materials not being *circulated* and determine: if they should be kept because they are useful; if they should be removed because their usefulness has ended, or how they could be put back into circulation.

(See chapter 1, Defining the Ministry, p. 15.)

Users

You must evaluate your library through the eyes of the users and potential users.

Do the people of the church *understand* what the library is all about? Are the *teachers* and *students* making use of the library?

Have you seen *changes in lives* because of the library ministry? What are you doing to guide people in their *reading habits*? Are there any *barriers* to the use of the library?

Ask a *cross section* of your church (all ages) why they come or don't come to your library.

(See in chapter 12, Remember the Needs of Readers, p. 171.)

Definitions

ACCESSION.   1. To enter the details of a book in a special ledger in the order of its acquisition for a permanent record.   2. The assigning of an identifying number (the accession number) to an item as it is added to the library collection. The number is taken from the sequential list of numbers found in the accession book.

ADDED ENTRY.   An entry into the library catalog other than the main entry or subject entry. Examples of added entries are title, series, and joint authors.

ANNOTATIONS.   A brief description of the contents of a book. This is part of the notes on the catalog card.

APPROPRIATIONS.   Money or materials given by an organization or an individual of the church for the development of the library.

AREA.   1. The space in the library room allotted for a special function.   2. A major section of the description on the catalog card such as the title and statement of authorship area, collation area, etc.

AUTHOR.   The person responsible for writing a book.

AUTHOR ENTRY.   The name of the author of a book used as the filing name in the catalog. Usually, for a book, this is the main entry.

BOOK CARD.   A card used to charge out a book or other material. The card identifies the item and borrower in the circulation records.

BOOK POCKET.   A prepared envelope that holds the book card while the book is in the library.

BROAD CLASSIFICATION. The grouping of books in classes or divisions without recognizing the more minute subdivisions.

CALL NUMBER. The number used to identify and locate a book or other material. For books it is composed of a classification number and the author's letters. It may also contain a symbol for a special location, a designation for edition, or a copy or volume number. For audiovisuals it is composed of a media symbol and an inventory number.

CATALOG. A library's listing of all material found in the library. Most church libraries list their materials on 3″ × 5″ cards according to a definite plan. A catalog records, describes, and indexes the resources of the library.

CATALOGER. A person who prepares the entries for the catalog. The information gleaned by her is usually put on a workslip from which a typist can prepare the necessary cards.

CATALOGING. Sometimes the word is used for the process involved in preparing books for the shelves and/or the process of making entries for the catalog.

CHARGING. The process of recording the loan of a book or other item for a patron. This involves obtaining the name of the borrower, providing the date the item is due in the library for both the library staff and the patron, placing the book card in its proper place for systematic follow up.

CLASS. 1. A subject group such as one of the 10 broad divisions of the Dewey Decimal System. 2. The number selected from the classification system to identify a specific group of books.

CLASSIFICATION. The art of arranging books or other materials according to a prepared scheme. In the process, books are grouped according to the same or similar subjects. Audio-visuals are grouped according to media.

CLASSIFICATION SCHEDULE.   A printed, logical arrangement of the whole field of knowledge.

CLOSE CLASSIFICATION.   Using the minute subdivisions of a classification schedule.

COLLATION.   A description of the physical condition of a book or other media. For books such information as the number of plates or the number of volumes, illustrations, book size, etc. can be included. For audio-visuals, such things as time involved for use and a technical description of the item are included.

COPYRIGHT.   The protection offered by the government to a publisher to protect against anyone else copying certain material for a specified number of years. The date a book is registered is the copyright date.

CROSS REFERENCE CARDS.   Inserted in the catalog to help people who do not use or are not acquainted with the subject wording the library uses. They direct from one heading to another. There are two kinds of cards—special reference cards and general reference cards.

DATE DUE SLIP.   A pre-printed paper form that is pasted in the library book to remind the borrower of the date the book should be back.

DESCRIPTIVE CATALOGING.   Involves determining the catalog entries that are to be made and getting the descriptive information needed for the catalog cards.

DICTIONARY CARD CATALOG.   A card catalog in which all the entries relating to books or other media are filed in two or more cabinets. Author and title cards may be in one set of drawers and the subject cards in another. Or there may be a separate set of drawers for each.

DUST JACKET. The paper cover a publisher puts on a hardback book for protection, information, and motivation to buy.

EDITION. A specific text of a published work. After an edition has been published, an author may make improvements by additions or deletions to the book. When printed again, the edition number will then change. A new edition differs from a reprint in that it implies changes or additions to the text.

END PAPER. The sheet of paper that is pasted to the inside of either the front or back cover of a book and to the inside edge of the first or last page of the book.

ENTRY WORD. The word, name, or phrase under which a card is filed in the catalog. Some entries are: the main entry (usually the author card), the title entry, and the subject entry.

GUIDE CARD. A 3″ × 5″ card with a projecting tab on which a letter, name, or term can be placed indicating what material follows.

HARDWARE. The term used to describe the equipment needed to properly use audio-visual equipment such as projectors, screens, and players.

HEADING. The word or phrase at the head of an entry used to indicate a special aspect of the media. Headings are made for subject content, series, title, etc.

IMPRINT. Information that has to do with the publication of a book or production of other media. Included are the date and place of publication and the name of the publisher.

INDENTATION. When typing catalog cards, three indentations are observed. Each indentation begins progressively farther from the left edge of the card.
The first indentation is sometimes called the author indentation and begins 10 spaces to the right of the edge.
The second indentation is sometimes called the title and paragraph indentation and begins 12 spaces to the right of the edge.

The third indentation is sometimes called the description indentation and begins 14 spaces to the right of the edge.

INSTRUCTIONAL MATERIALS CENTER.   A descriptive name for the library indicating that all learning materials are kept here and are available to be borrowed, or used in the room by teachers and pupils alike.

JOINT AUTHOR/EDITOR.   A person partially responsible for the content of a book.

LIBRARY OF CONGRESS CARD.   For each book received at the Library of Congress, a catalog card is made for their use containing a description of the book as well as a Library of Congress and Dewey Decimal notation. These cards are printed and made available in sets to other libraries at a minimum cost.

MAIN ENTRY.   The basic catalog entry; for books it is usually the author entry. This card carries a complete record of information used to identify the book. In addition there is a record of all other entries made for the book called tracings. For audio-visuals the main entry card is usually the title entry.

MATERIAL.   An all-inclusive term used to describe any item found in the library. This includes audio-visuals as well as printed media.

MEDIA.   Printed or audio-visual forms of communication and any necessary equipment required to render them usable.

NOTATION.   A system of numbers and/or letters used to represent an item in the classification scheme.

NOTE.   A phrase or sentence that may be placed in the third paragraph of the catalog card to explain the history or content of the book and indicate if a bibliography appears in the book. Each note is in a separate paragraph.

PAMPHLET. A publication of less than 50 pages usually on one specific subject.

PERIODICAL. A publication released at regular intervals such as a magazine or catalog.

POLICY. A written plan to assist in the proper management of the library.

PROCESSING. The work of acquiring, cataloging, and preparing library materials.

REFERENCE BOOK. A book which can only be used in the library and is kept in a special area. Books in this category include Bible encyclopedias, Bible dictionaries, Bible concordances, etc.

RESOURCE CENTER. A descriptive name for the library indicating that the library is a place where the communicating resources of the church are stored and distributed.

SATELLITE LIBRARY. A small selection of library materials stored, displayed, and circulated in an area of the church campus that is more convenient for people to use than coming to the main library.

"SEE ALSO" REFERENCE CARD. A card which refers from a subject term which *has been used* in the catalog, to other terms which are related to it and under which additional information may be found.

"SEE" REFERENCE CARDS. A card which refers from a subject term *not used* to one which has the same meaning and can be found in the catalog.

SERIES. Separate books, issued at different times under one title.

SHELF LIST. A file containing 3" × 5" cards for each book in the library. The cards are arranged in the same order as they appear on the shelves. The front side of the card duplicates the main entry card, while the back can be used to record other information usually found on accession sheets and thereby eliminate a record on sheets.

SOFTWARE. The term used to describe the media used with audio-visual equipment. This includes such things as filmstrips, cassettes, transparencies, etc.

STACKS. Usually free standing shelves on which books are stored.

SUBJECT. The theme or topic treated by an author in his book.

SUBJECT AUTHORITY FILE. A record of each subject heading used by the cataloger. Included in it are also the "see" and "see also" references made for each subject heading. The file is maintained in order to have uniform terms.

SUBJECT CATALOGING. Involves assigning subject headings and classification numbers to books.

SUBJECT ENTRY. The filing word or phrase used in a catalog entry. It is referred to as the subject heading.

SUBJECT HEADING. A word or phrase which expresses the theme or topic of a book. All books dealing with the same subject use the same subject heading.

SUBJECT WORDING. Wording a classifier uses to describe a certain subject.

TITLE. 1. The official name of a book. 2. The title statement on the catalog card will include the alternative title, subtitle or other associated descriptive matters.

TRACING. The record on the main entry card which includes additional headings under which the book is represented in the library.

Helpful Titles and Addresses

Akers' Simple Library Cataloging 16th Ed.
Arthur Curley/Jana Varlejs
The Scarecrow Press, Inc.
Metuchen, N.J. 1977
Simplified ideas for cataloging, especially for small libraries.

American Library Association
Public Information Office
50 E. Huron, Chicago, Ill. 60611
Helpful information on public libraries. Adaptations
can be made for church libraries.

Books for Christian Educators 1966
Evangelical Teacher Training Assn.
110 Bridge, Wheaton, Ill. 60187
Listing of Christian education books

Bro-Dart Industries
P.O. Box 92337
World Way Postal Center
Los Angeles, Calf. 90009 or
1609 Memorial Avenue
Williamsport, Penn. 17701
Library supplies not available in your local Christian bookstore.

The Care and Repair of Printed Materials
Broadman Press, Nashville, Tenn. 1970
To help keep your books in good repair.

The Children's Book Council
175 5th Avenue
New York, N.Y. 10010

Church Library Deskbook
Broadman Press, Nashville, Tenn. 1965

Church Library Manual, Leona L. Althoff
Convention Press, Nashville, Tenn. 1955

Church Library Handbook
La Vose Newton
Multnomah Press, Portland, Ore. 1972
Helpful information for church libraries just beginning.

Church Resource Library
Maryann J. Dotts
Abingdon Press, 1976
"How to start it and make it grow."
Abbreviated subject heading list.

Commonsense Cataloging 2nd Ed.
Esther J. Piercy, Rev. Marion Sanner
H.W. Wilson, New York 1974
"A manual for the organization of books and other
materials in schools and small public libraries.

Decimal Classification and Relative Index
Melvil Dewey—3 Vol. 18th Ed.
Lake Placid Club, N.Y.
Forest Press, Inc. of Lake Placid Club
Educational Foundation 1971
Official Dewey Decimal

Demco Educational Corporation
Fresno Calif., or
Box 7488, Madison, Wis.
Library supplies not available in your local
Christian bookstore

Developing Multi-Media Libraries
Warren B. Hicks/Alma M. Tillin
R.R. Bowker Co., N.Y. 1970
Overview of audio-visual materials and practical
procedures for cataloging audio-visuals.

Effective Library Exhibits
Kate Koplan
Oceana Publications, N.Y.
Ideas to help promote books

Evangelical Church Library Association
Box 353, Glen Ellyn, Ill. 60137
Quarterly publication: Librarian's World Magazine.

Gaylord Brother, Inc.
29 N. Aurora Street, Stockton, Calif., or
Syracuse, N.Y.
Library supplies not available in your local Christian bookstore. Publish
booklet: Organization of the Small Library.

The Highsmith Company, Inc.
Fort Atkinson, Wis.
Library supplies not available in your local Christian bookstore.

Honey for a Child's Heart
• Gladys Hunt
Zondervan Publications
Grand Rapids, Mich. 1969
Use and selection of Christian books for children.

Inland Lutheran Library Association
Riverside County, Calif.
Meet annually in February for fellowship and instruction.

Introduction to Library Services
Aline C. Wisdom
McGraw Hill, Inc.
New York 1974
Overall picture of the public library from which
ideas can be culled for the church library.

Key to Successful Church Library Rev. Ed.
Erwin E. John
Augsburg Publications,
Minneapolis, Minn. 1967

The Library and Resource Center in Christian Education
Betty McMichael
Moody Press, Chicago, Ill. 1977
Appendix 4—Subject headings for church libraries.

Library of Congress
Catalog Distribution Service Division
Building 159, Navy Yard Annex
Washington, D.C., 20541
Information on Library of Congress unit cards.

Media
127 9th Avenue North
Nashville, Tenn. 37203
Quarterly church library magazine by the Southern Baptist Convention.

The Minister's Library
Cyril J. Barber
Baker Book House, Grand Rapids, Mich. 1974

National Library Week
One Park Avenue, New York, N.Y. 10805
Send for brochures and prices concerning
National Library Week in April.

Pacific Northwest Association of Church Libraries
Box Sect. 12379, Seattle, Wash. 98111
Area church library fellowship and instruction.

Promoting Your Church Library
Marian S. Johnson
Augsburg Publishing,
Minneapolis, Minn. 1968

Successful Church Libraries
Elmer J. Towns/Cyril J. Barber
Baker Book House, Grand Rapids, Mich. 1971

Sears List of Subject Headings 11th Ed.
Minnie E. Sears, Edited by Barbara M. Westby
H.B. Wilson, N.Y. 1977
Extensive subject heading list.

200 (Religion) Class—Dewey Decimal Classification 18th Ed.
Melvil Dewey
Broadman Press, Nashville, Tenn. 1966
200 class schedule—a must for church library catalogers.

Index

---

*See definitions